M000012607

Table of Contents

Part I What Business is Right for You?

Part II How to Start the Business

Part III How to Keep the Business Successful

Part IV Step-by-Step

National Nurses in Business Association, Inc.
Copyright ©

Self-Employed RN:
How to become a self-employed RN and/or business owner

Third Edition

First edition published under the title
Business Training for RNs

Written by Patricia Ann Bemis, RN CEN

President
National Nurses in Business Association, Inc.

Published in the United States by the
National Nurses in Business Association, Inc.

Published by

National Nurses in Business Association, Inc.
Post Office Box 561081
Rockledge, FL 32156-1081 USA.

http://www.nnba.net

Cover graphic design and photography: Warren Bemis

Copyright 2011

ISBN print edition

978-0-9678112-5-3

Foreword—Note from the President

The opportunities for nurses are changing. We now have the opportunity to start a business of our own. We are no longer enslaved to the hospital to make a living. We can be self-employed or a business owner, we have the opportunity to gain respect as true professionals and the opportunity to create wealth for ourselves.

This book is written and published in the hope that more nurses will learn about their options and become independent.

The association, founded in 1985, is the #1 professional association for nurse entrepreneurs:

- providing information on new and traditional RN self-employment;
- offering business education to start and operate a self-employment venture;
- acting as a national voice;
- maintaining a national networking arena since 1985.

The NNBA can be your support team, resource consultant, networking hub, and business coach.

Look at our website online at http://www.nnba.net or call 1-877-353-8888 for more information.

Patricia Ann Bemis, RN, CEN
President
National Nurses in Business Association, Inc.

Warning—Disclaimer

This book is designed to provide information on business opportunities for nurses. It is sold with the understanding that the publisher and authors are not engaged in rendering legal, accounting, or other professional services. If legal or other expert assistance is required, the services of a competent professional should be sought.

It is not the purpose of this book to provide all the information available on business training or to present all the varied opportunities available to nurses. You are urged to read all the information to learn more about entrepreneurship and tailor the information to your unique needs.

Nurse entrepreneurship is not a get-rich quick scheme. Anyone who decides to start and operate his or her own business must expect to invest a lot of time and effort into the business. For most nurses, nurse entrepreneurship is a lucrative career option.

Every effort has been made to make this book as accurate as possible. However, there may be mistakes, both typographical and in content. Therefore, this book is a general guide and not the ultimate source of business information. The book contains information only current up to the publishing date.

The purpose of this book is to entertain, empower, and educate. The author and the National Nurses in Business Association, Inc. shall have neither liability nor responsibility to any person or entity with respect to any loss or damage caused, or alleged to have been caused, directly or indirectly, by the information contained in this book.

Any people or organizations mentioned herein are believed to be reputable. The National Nurses in Business Association, Inc. or any of its employees accept no responsibility for the activities of those mentioned or endorse any of their products.

Part I:

What Business is Right for You?

Chapter 1
Introduction

Welcome. This book is designed for registered nurses who are interested in gaining respect and earning a higher income by becoming self-employed or owning a business. With this book, you will learn how to decide what self-employment or small business choice is right for you, how to get the venture started, and how to keep it successful.

Wouldn't it be wonderful if all you needed to start a business was a great idea? Wouldn't it be wonderful if you didn't have to worry about naming, writing a business plan, negotiating contracts, bookkeeping, and taxes? Wouldn't it be wonderful if all we had to do were to complete tasks we enjoyed and then sit back and be creative all day?

In the real world, you must learn a ton of information about legal, financial, and documentation issues. You have to run the office, do the errands, get the mail, answer the phone, do the bookkeeping, run the meetings, and document everything involved with running a business. A profitable, smooth-running business is almost always preceded by careful preparation. This book is part of that preparation.

Estimates vary, but generally there are more than 29.3 million non-farm small businesses in the U.S. What are you waiting for?

Author

My name is Patricia Ann Bemis. I am an experienced nurse entrepreneur and president of the National Nurses in Business Association. I speak and write on clinical and business topics. I am an informational entrepreneur, national speaker, and published author. My clinical work, *Emergency Nursing Bible*, was written in 1998 and is currently in its fifth edition.

When I started my self-employment venture, my business knowledge was practically nonexistent. In fact, what little business knowledge I had was misdirected by my nursing education. I had developed a mindset that prevented me from looking at the possibility of making it on my own. I had come to believe that nursing was only about caring and not about money. I was wrong.

Nursing is about earning money to support yourself and your family. It is about money. You can't survive without money. The service you provide to earn that money is about caring.

In this book, I will pass on what I have learned. I will guide you to a highly rewarding independent nursing career.

Chapter 2
History of Nurse
Entrepreneurs

This chapter presents a brief history of the nurses involved at the onset of nurse entrepreneurship and outlines the evolution of nurse entrepreneurship over the recent past.

The Art of Nursing

The art of nursing is a talent that can be identified in nurses from the past and present. Nurses can be found in pre-Christian centuries and throughout history as primitive mothers, wise women, goddesses, monks, and sisters of religious organizations.

Laura Gasparis Vonfrolio defines the intangible art of nursing as, "The intangible gift of nursing is the ability to connect with our patients and transfer positive energy, the therapeutic use of the self to heal and nurture, and the ability to create an interpersonal bond that is conducive to healing."

Florence Nightingale

The first secular nursing training was started by Florence Nightingale (1820-1910) in England in 1854. Despite chronic brucellosis, which left her severely disabled, she made a worldwide change in health care. Her statistical data collections regarding disease, death, and sanitary conditions contributed to hospital reform and standards. The knowledge-based Nightingale School of Nursing was not associated with a church, focused on patient care, and initiated a system to monitor nurses' performance. Unfortunately, little regard was given to the importance of a nurse's work and they were considered secular servant nurses and paid the same wages as the servants of the day.

Mary Grant Seacole

Mary Grant Seacole (1805-1881) a freeborn black Jamaican born in Kingston, Jamaica, learned folk medicine from her mother and volunteered her services in the Crimean war effort. The Nightingale School of Nursing and the governing military forces rejected her. Undaunted, she started a hotel where the wounded soldiers on both sides of the conflict could recover. Nightingale's accomplishments overshadowed Seacole's and her medical knowledge as a healer raised fears that she would not be subservient.

Clara Barton

Clara (Clarissa Harlow) Barton (1821-1912) began her career during the Civil War and she was soon nicknamed the Angle of the Battlefield. She established the Bureau of Records of Missing Army Men at her own expense to help families find their loved ones. In 1881, she founded the American National Red Cross.

She retired in 1904 at the age of 83. Barton said of the Red Cross, "It is a peculiar institution, without nationality, race, creed or sect, embracing the entire world in its humanizing bond of brotherhood, without arbitrary laws or rules, and yet stronger than armies and higher than thrones."

Evolution

Nursing continued to evolve and during times of peace, many nurses turned to private duty nursing. They were self-employed and provided nursing services to patients either in the hospital or in the patient's home. They selected the hours and the cases they would work. Eventually, independence and self-employment gained them respect as professionals.

After the depression in 1929, nurses were forced back to their alma maters, the hospital, to find work. Patients and families could no longer afford to pay the private duty nurses. At times of military conflict, the nurse enjoyed increased popularity as a hard worker dedicated to her profession, but the public image of the independent professional never returned. A few self-employed, private duty nurses lasted well up into the 1950s. As payment for healthcare became the responsibility of the insurance companies, the self-employed nurse all but disappeared.

In the 1970s, nurses began to alter their nursing career paths by developing businesses and consulting services that stepped out of the traditional mold. Karon Gibson, RN, started a nursing agency, American Nurse, in Chicago, a first of its kind. Laura Gasparis Vonfrolio, RN, developed her company, Education Enterprises, in New York. She provided CPR training to businesses. By 1980, Clarissa Russo, RN, from Southern California, started presenting seminars nationally addressing career options and business opportunities for nurses. Russo, by her example, proved that nurse entrepreneurship was possible and financially feasible.

During the 1970s and early 1980s, corporate America found it increasingly difficult to make a profit and looked for ways to cut expenses. Businesses began to lay off employees, cut benefit packages, and do whatever was necessary to increase profits. Healthcare facilities, as part of corporate America, were also trying to make a profit and followed the lead of other companies and cut payroll. As a result, many positions were deleted and whole departments removed from the healthcare corporate structure.

Many nurses were innovators of change and as the hospitals cut services, new areas of consulting arose. At the same time, insurance companies were looking for ways to help their adjustors understand the medical problems, obtain the appropriate medical care, and decrease the disability. The decreased disability was worth less money for maintaining the claimant or when settling the claim based on the severity of the disability. In the early 1970s, the insurance companies looked to nurses to fill this much-needed role for rehabilitation and states also looked to nurses to work with workers' compensation cases. These nurses were called rehabilitation nurses or workers' compensation nurses and their work included what is now called legal nurse consulting, case management, care management, and aspects of life care planning.

At the same time, nurses and nurse attorneys were pioneering the field of bringing nursing expertise to attorneys and insurance companies when judging the merits of a case based on the adherence of the medical care to the standards-of-care in the U.S. The role of the legal nurse consultant grew rapidly.

The education department of healthcare facilities suffered the greatest losses. However, education was still needed on an intermittent basis and consultants filled this need. Paying a consultant to do the same service as a full-time employee made good sense since paying the consultant cost less than the full time employee wages. This was a cost-effective way of doing business.

Laid-off nurses and healthcare workers set up consulting services. They often found themselves working for the same hospital that forced them out. Outsourcing (sending work to an outside provider in order to cut costs) is considered one of the best methods to decrease expenses and increase profits.

By the mid 1980s, nurse consultants were practicing in many areas. Individual nurses were developing fields of consulting that never existed in the past. They were selling their services to healthcare facilities, attorneys, and insurance companies.

In 1985, it became evident that nurse entrepreneurs needed a support and networking system. David Norris, a male critical-care nurse in Petaluma, California, foresaw the need to support nurses in business. He started a newsletter to promote and support nurses in business and the National Nurses in Business Association was begun. By 1989, the association was serving nurses across the country as it continues to do today.

The National Nurses in Business Association, Inc. (NNBA) is the pioneer association dedicated to promoting and supporting nurses in business. It provides nurses information on business startup that gives them the confidence to continue when they thought there was no way to succeed. The NNBA makes available to nurse entrepreneurs the collective wisdom and practical suggestions of many successful nurses. Gross income for some NNBA members exceeds 35-million dollars annually.

Currently, nurse entrepreneurs are often hired to:

- use their nursing knowledge to increase proficiency of staff nurses;
- identify and resolve problems;
- supplement staff;
- act as a mechanism for change;
- do pre-survey assessments;
- provide impartiality;
- train;
- make recommendations that the facility does not want to take accountability for;
- bring new life to a facility or department;
- create a new department;
- influence employees;
- review patient care;
- analyze patient care;
- plan patient care.

Conclusion

This chapter identified a few of the early nurse entrepreneurs and described the evolution of nurse entrepreneurship briefly. Nurse entrepreneurship is constantly changing and evolving as new rules, laws, and technical changes are adopted. The economy of business continues to play a significant role in nursing. Use this information to understand the past. The past has a significant impact on the present and future.

Chapter 3
Industry Projections

Industry projections are used to guide career plans. This chapter will identify projections to be considered when planning your career path as a nurse entrepreneur.

Fastest Growing

Management, scientific, healthcare, and technical consulting services are projected to be the fastest growing industries. According to *Modern Healthcare*, when most sectors were losing jobs, healthcare added jobs.

Among all the occupations, healthcare is expected to grow and make up 10 of the 20 fastest growing occupations in the country. Businesses will continue to outsource and hire temporary help in the future making self-employment realistic and profitable. The following projections should be considered when deciding what industry to enter.

- The U.S. will need 1.2 million RNs by 2014 (resource RN January 2009 pg. 17).

- Professional and business services are expected to grow.
- Education and health services are projected to grow faster and add more jobs than any other sector. About 1 out of 4 jobs created will be either healthcare, social assistance, or private education services.
- The information sector is expected to grow rapidly. This includes software publishing, Internet publishing, broadcasting, and service providers; web search portals and data processing services.
- Overall employment in leisure and hospitality is expected to grow.
- Government facilities, including schools and hospitals, are expected to increase.
- Women-owned businesses that receive government contracts are expected to have an advantage over the general public.

Technology

Technology is another key factor when looking at future employment trends. New technology can create new opportunities and eliminate others. The Internet has created great demand for workers in the information and technology fields and decreased the demand for others, e.g., travel agents, because people can now purchase their own services online.

Reducing healthcare fraud is a priority of federal law enforcement. One of the goals is to decrease Medicare costs by identifying fraud. For example, nurses are being hired for the recovery audit contractor (RAC) program. There are potential opportunities on both sides of the issue.

Population

The U.S. population is anticipated to increase. Growth means more customers looking for goods and services. The age group born in the years from 1945 to 1965 (baby boomers) will increase by 43.6% or 11.5 million persons, more than any other group.

In the future, minorities and immigrants are expected to constitute a larger share of the labor force. The number of Hispanics is projected to continue to grow much faster than other racial and ethnic groups. The number of women is expected to grow at a faster rate than men.

Shift from Products to Service

The long-term shift from goods (products) to services is anticipated to continue. Service jobs are expected to account for most of the new jobs generated.

Conclusion

When considering a self-employment or small business venture, it is important to design the company with the future in mind.

Chapter 4:
Four Basic Steps to
Starting a Business

According to the Small Business Administration (SBA), there are four basic steps to developing the information you need to start a small business. This chapter lists those steps. Don't be concerned if you can't answer all the questions of this exercise. The information needed will be provided later in this book.

1. List your reasons for wanting to go into business. Some of the most common reasons for starting a business are:
    a. self-management;
    b. financial independence;
    c. creative freedom;
    d. full use of personal skills and knowledge.
2. Next determine what business is right for you. Ask yourself these questions:

    a. What do I like to do with my time?

    b. What technical skills have I learned or developed?

    c. What do others say I am good at?

    d. Will I have the support of my family?

    e. How much time do I have to run a successful business?

    f. Do I have any hobbies or interests that are marketable?

3. Identify your business niche. Research and answer these questions:

    a. What business interests me?

    b. What services or products will I sell?

    c. Is my idea practical and will it fill a need?

    d. What is my competition?

    e. What is my business's advantage over existing firms?

    f. Can I deliver a better quality service?

    g. Can I create a demand for my business?

4. The final step before developing your plan is the pre-business checklist. You should answer these questions:

    a. What skills and experience do I bring to the business?

    b. What legal structure will I use?

    c. How will my company's business records be maintained?

    d. What insurance coverage will be needed?

    e. What equipment or supplies will I need?

    f. How will I compensate myself?

    g. What are my resources?

    h. What financing will I need?

    i. Where will my business be located?

j.   What will I name my business?

Conclusion

In order to complete the exercise in this chapter, you will need information that is provided later in this book. When complete, this exercise will help you create a focused, well-researched plan. It will serve as a blueprint for business operations, management, and capitalization. The NNBA offers full service assistance on business plans, including templates, seminars, training sessions, and home study courses on DVD.

Chapter 5
Self-Employment Facts

Dale Carnegie said, "Without the facts, you will stew around in a state of confusion." This chapter provides the facts a nurse needs to know regarding self-employment.

Fact #1: Self-employment opportunities are unlimited for a nurse.

As a nurse, your self-employment opportunities are unlimited. Your method of choosing a new career is the same as outlined by career counselors. The advantage is that you are a nurse, highly skilled, college educated, and talented. Your new career may not bear any resemblance to your old nursing job of providing patient care, but it will build on your current knowledge and skills.

Fact #2: You can start part-time.

You can start part-time, keep your current employment and benefits, and learn how it feels to be independent. When the time is right, you will be ready to move to self-employment if it is for you. In the meantime, you will feel better about yourself, your frustrations will decrease, and you will have freed your creative spirit.

Fact #3: Daydreaming is good

The National Nurses in Business Association suggests you make a list of what you enjoyed doing in past jobs and hobbies. When you look over your list, often you'll remember one or more tasks as more enjoyable than others.

When you decide what you enjoy or are even passionate about, design a job (make it up) that includes the experiences that you find rewarding and fulfilling. Develop a detailed job description, including pay scale, work environment, location, and daily tasks. The next step is to match your personalized dream job with those in the real world. You may have to create your business or it may already exist.

Fact #4: Nurses often sort through many self-employment ideas.

Most nurse entrepreneurs sort through many ideas before they come upon the one that is right for them. The following is a list of roles performed by self-employed nurses.

- Nurses who identify problems, develop workable solutions, and resolve problems for healthcare facilities. Examples of nurses who do this type of work are:
    - clinical consultants starting new specialty areas;

- o   experts at cost-cutting maneuvers;
- o   auditors and investigators of billing fraud;
- o   mock surveyors.

- Nurses who offer medical and nursing education to patients, families, healthcare professionals, and healthcare facilities. Examples of nurses who do this type of work are:
  - o   teachers and educators who design and present programs;
  - o   trainers who present pre-designed programs, such as CPR, ACLS, TNCC, etc.
  - o   authors, writers, and small press publishing companies.

- Nurses who design customized care plans and initiate treatment for patients to promote wellness. Examples of nurses who do this type of work are:
  - o   owners of wellness clinics;
  - o   wellness coaches;
  - o   holistic nurses.

- Nurses who offer temporary healthcare staffing service (nursing agency/registry) to healthcare facilities (hospitals, nursing homes, correctional facilities, etc.).

- Nurses who offer temporary companion care staffing services (non-medical, private pay) to patients in their homes.

- Nurses who provide durable medical equipment, medical supplies, and/or medical clothing (uniforms and scrubs).

- Nurses who review the care provided and develop new ways to ensure the patient's well being and safety. Examples of nurses who do this type of work are:
  - care managers (aging in place);
  - case managers;
  - patient advocates.

- Nurses who provide an insider's view on medical issues to legal professionals. Examples of nurses who do this type of work are:
  - legal nurse consultants;
  - forensic nurses;
  - life care planners;
  - Medicare set-aside service providers.

- Nurses who bring new products to market.

Fact #5: Clinical nursing options are limited.

Clinical nursing services may be offered, but they are limited because many services need a physician's order and obtaining payment is difficult. Patients usually expect insurance (private, Medicare, Medicaid) to pay for nursing care. Insurance companies do not typically pay for care provided by an RN.

Fact #6: Self-employed nurses need to acquire business knowledge.

Nurses are skilled at providing professional and technical services. Unfortunately, these skills and knowledge are NOT the same as the skills and knowledge needed to start and operate a business.

Fact #7: Self-employed nurses need to learn terms.

The term *consultant* is a generic term describing a

person who offers expert or professional advice to clients. It is not a legal term. *Independent contractor* is the legal term used for tax purposes by consultants.

Fact #8: Self-employment requires that you start a business.

Self-employment, in any form, requires that you start a business. Viable options for nurses include starting the business as a sole proprietor, limited liability company, or corporation.

Fact #9: A business is a legal entity.

All businesses are independent legal entities governed by state and federal laws. First and foremost, starting a business is about seeking out the laws that pertain to your business and then creating a business that is lawful and profitable. Not following the law is a criminal act. Criminal acts are punishable by law.

Fact #10: Nurses often start before they are ready.

Nurses often acquire customers before their business procedures and financial systems are in place. This can be a costly mistake. Learning and developing business procedures and financial systems BEFORE the business opens is ideal.

Fact #11: Certain tasks are common to all businesses.

ALL businesses are responsible for the following tasks.

- Registering the business in a state as a legal entity. In most states it is a criminal act to operate a business within the state without registering with the state. If your business offers services as outlined in your nurse practice act, you may already be registered to practice in your state.

- Obtaining an employer identification number (EIN) from the federal government as your business tax reporting number. In some situations, your social security number may be used.

- Completing state and federal filings at specific intervals.

- Filing for and paying licenses and permits related to the industry.

- Collecting, reporting, and paying the state sales tax collected from individuals.

- Keeping financial documentation of all income and tax-deductible expenses, reporting it to state and federal governments quarterly, and paying taxes. Methods of accounting and the date of fiscal year-end are regulated by law and can vary with the type of legal structure of the business.

- Paying payroll taxes, unemployment insurance, and workers' compensation.

- Filing quarterly statements regarding payroll to the state and federal governments.

- Complying with requirements unique to your individual city, county, and/or state.

Fact #12: Medical terms and business terms are often different.

The term *nursing agency* is medical lingo. The correct industry classification is *temporary staffing* or *help service*. Starting a healthcare temporary staffing ser-

How to Become a Self-Employed RN and/or Business Owner

vice requires knowledge of the industry and the rules and requirements of federal, state, and local governments. Because the industry has its roots in the 1890s, protocols are well established. Increase your chance of success by learning the industry from business experts.

Starting a nursing agency is a complex process that is often made more difficult by poorly written manuals and guidebooks providing misinformation. Reliable information can be found at the National Nurses in Business Association.

Fact #13: Understanding terminology is often difficult.

In the U.S., the word entrepreneur has at least two definitions.

1. The purest view defines entrepreneurs as those few people who generate new, revolutionary business ideas and grow the idea into high-growth businesses. These entrepreneurs are the driving force behind new ideas that create new jobs.

2. The current common view defines a small business owner as an entrepreneur. Most dictionary definitions follow this common viewpoint of a person who organizes a business, operates the business, and takes on the financial risk of doing so.

Is this distinction important? I think so. The true entrepreneurs need to be fostered in our economy because they are the strength behind our business economy. For the purpose of this book, the word entrepreneur is used as any person who takes on the role of business owner or becomes self-employed.

Fact #14: You don't have to start from scratch.

Starting a business, part time or full time, doesn't necessarily mean developing the idea and building the company from scratch. You can buy an existing business, purchase a franchise or a business opportunity, or become an independent retailer for another company.

Buying an existing business is often more costly than building a business. However, it may offer you an established reputation and a customer base. You don't have to invent the wheel so to speak. If you are interested in buying a business, talk with the NNBA.

If buying a business is not what you want and you want a little more help getting started and operating the business, a franchise might be right for you. Many well-known franchise companies have a ready-made customer base. Basically you, the franchisee, pay the franchiser an initial fee and ongoing royalties. How much you receive in support varies with each company as well as the cost.

Affiliate programs are, in a broad sense, any type of revenue-sharing program where an affiliate receives a portion of income for delivering sales, leads, or traffic to a merchant. Affiliate programs can be online.

A business opportunity is a packaged business investment that allows you to start the business. Unlike a franchise, the business opportunity exercises no control over you or your company. There is no continuing relationship. This is good if you want an in-road to starting your business and refuse to give up your freedom.

Types of Opportunities	Description
Cooperatives	An existing business that allows another similar business to affiliate with it and others, usually in a network of similar businesses.
Dealers	Individuals who purchase the right to sell products put out by other companies, such as vitamins or holistic medicines. The individual is often advertised as an authorized dealer. A distributor sells to dealers and a dealer sells directly to customers. The terms are often used interchangeably.
Licensees	Individuals who purchase the right to use the sellers trade name and certain methods, equipment, or product lines.
Multi-level marketing	This is very popular with individuals looking for a part-time, flexible business. The best known are Avon, Tupperware, and Mary Kay Cosmetics. Typically the individual purchases a sample kit and receives the opportunity to sell directly to family, friends, and personal contacts. Not all states regulate multi-level marketing.

| Vending machines | An individual who contracts with a vending machine company. The company provides the machines and the locations; the individual restocks them and collects the money. |

Fact #15: Support is available.

Self-employed nurses elevate their career to its highest pinnacle: independence. They gain self-respect and create the opportunity to create wealth. The National Nurses in Business Association is a membership organization that offers the support needed to bridge the gap between nursing and business.

Fact #16: Some businesses are considered recession proof.

Goals set by governments and large organizations, such as the American Association of Retired Persons (AARP), American Medical Association (AMA), American Nursing Association (ANA), and the American Bar Association (ABA) have a powerful influence on the business world and wield influence over the minds of their many individual members. Businesses that provide services to meet these goals have a high rate of success just based on the sheer numbers of individuals involved. Because these services may be needed even in a failing economy, they are considered recession proof.

Fact #17: Regulatory changes can bring about new business ideas.

New knowledge often brings about industry changes. Regulations are often put in place to regulate the industry changes. Nurse entrepreneurs who are the first to implement businesses that address or provide services to meet these new regulations have a high rate of success. For example, a new regulation was put in place in Pennsylvania requiring long term care facilities to collect statistics and report to the state on infection rates in their facilities. No such statistics had ever been collected by these facilities. They had no procedure in place and employed no nurses who knew how to collect and report the statistics. A certified infection control nurse started a new business that provided services to collect these statistics and report them to the state for the facilities. Her business was a great success.

Conclusion

It can be concluded that with these facts you can develop a clear picture and not stew around in a state of confusion.

Chapter 6
Is Self-Employment for You?

Self employment is not for everyone. This chapter lists the rewards of nurse self-employment and the advantages nurses have over the general public when starting a self-employment venture. It also contains a quiz to determine if you have the personality type to excel in business.

Rewards

Rewards of being self-employed are making decisions without input from your employer. Are making the following decisions important for you?

- Why you will work (to maintain your lifestyle or a philanthropic goal)

- Who you will work with

- What you will do (patient care, chart review, sell a product, write a book, be a speaker, be a consultant, etc.)

- When you will do the work (days, night, weekends, early in the day or late at night; you decide)

- Where you will work (in your home, in an upscale office building, in your patient's home)

- How you will do the work (your way)

- How much you will charge for your services

Advantages

Nurses often have advantages over the general public at succeeding in a business venture. Are these advantages applicable to you?

Advantage	Rationale
Nurses have a college education with a large knowledge base.	A nurse's knowledge includes medicine, pharmacology, physical and respiratory therapy, teaching, spiritual and holistic medicine, nutrition, biology, physiology, and record keeping to name a few.
The majority of nurses are women.	According to the Small Business Administration, business ownership is the most effective means of improving a women's economic well being.

Nurses have a dependable income.	Hospital jobs provide ideal financial support during business startup with weekend, night, and part-time scheduling. Many part-time and weekend positions also provide insurance and retirement benefits that are helpful during startup.
Nurses are highly skilled.	The United States Department of Labor identified eight universal job skills in a past edition of their *Occupational Outlook Handbook*. The skills are leadership/persuasion, problem solving, teamwork, manual dexterity, instructing others, intuition, frequent public contact, and physical stamina. Each occupation in the handbook requires a variety of these skills, commonly four or less. Nursing requires all eight skills. Therefore, nurses can do any job in the United States including being an owner operator of a small business.

The nursing process is the same as the business process.	The process steps are to collect data, analyze the data, develop a plan, implement the plan, evaluate the outcome, revise the plan, implement the plan, evaluate the outcome, and repeat the process. Nurses are experienced and proficient with this business process.
Nurses are in short supply and in great demand	Educational facilities have been unable to produce the number of nurses needed.
Nurses are talented.	Few nurses realize that they have a talent like any great artist that emotionally demands they practice their art. That talent is the intangible art of nursing. Artists often put up with great adversity to practice their art–giving up food for paint or playing their music in dim-lit saloons without pay. The nurse views herself as a nurse practicing the art and science of nursing. The healthcare facility views the nurse as a labor force to perform tasks and does not recognize the art of nursing. That lack of insight by the healthcare facility creates a fundamental problem.

How to Become a Self-Employed RN and/or Business Owner

RNs are registered to practice within their state.	State nurse practice acts for registered nurses do not prohibit self-employment. Any registered nurse can be self-employed or a business owner including two-year graduates and diploma nurses. No advance degrees are necessary unless your business includes diagnosing and treating medical problems.

Personality Type Quiz

The following personality type quiz may help you decide if self-employment is right for you. Ask yourself several questions and answer them honestly. Don't spend too such time on the questions; just answer yes or no quickly. The yes answers indicate that chances are good that you will be successful in your business venture. If you have a lot of no answers, it may mean that self-employment may not be compatible with your personality type.

1. Is making your own decisions important to you?

    a. Yes

    b. No

2. Do you enjoy change?

    a. Yes

    b. No

3. Do you enjoy competing?

    a. Yes

    b. No

4. Do you deal well with stress?

    a. Yes

    b. No

5. Do you have a network of people you can tap for assistance?

    a. Yes

    b. No

6. Is this venture compatible with your life and career goals?

    a. Yes

    b. No

7. Do you have sufficient money if you don't get paid on a regular basis?

    a. Yes

    b. No

8. Do you have a strong drive to succeed as an independent contractor?

    a. Yes

    b. No

9. Do you like the idea of being your own boss?

    a. Yes

    b. No

10. Do you have a strong self-image with solid self-esteem?

a. Yes

b. No

11. Are you ready to learn how to start and manage a profitable business?

a. Yes

b. No

12. Are you willing to keep track of and pay your own business expenses?

a. Yes

b. No

13. Are you willing to pay your own income taxes quarterly and pay your own benefits, such as liability and health insurance and retirement costs?

a. Yes

b. No

Conclusion

Based on the information learned from this chapter, it can be concluded that self-employment is a personal choice based on your personal situation, talent, temperament, and financial status. Self-employment may not be for all nurses. Is self-employment right for you?

Chapter 7
Specialties and
Related Self-Employment Ideas

Nurses tend to look at their skills in categories of specialty. This chapter lists nursing specialty areas, defines the care given, defines the typical employer, and offers some self-employment ideas. The specialties are presented alphabetically.

Ambulatory Care Nursing

Ambulatory care nurses treat patients of all ages with acute and chronic illnesses and injuries on an outpatient basis.

Care includes:
- triage;
- patient education;
- pain management;
- case management;
- discharge planning to restore, maintain, and promote the patients' physical well being.

Telehealth Nursing Practice (TNP) is a subspecialty.

The Telehealth Nursing Practice Standards define Telehealth Nursing Practice as nursing practice using the nursing process to provide care for individual patients or defined patient populations over the phone or other electronic communication media.

Ambulatory care nurses are typically employed by healthcare facilities and clinics.

Self-employment ideas include:

- consulting;
- teaching;
- operating a placement agency or staffing agency;
- providing the services of nurses and other personnel to the ambulatory care facility.

Cardiac Rehabilitation Nursing

Cardiac rehabilitation nurses treat older adults with coronary artery disease who are making lifestyle changes to prevent worsening of the disease after surgical intervention.

Care includes:
- consulting and teaching;
- heart monitoring during physical workouts;
- teaching lifestyle changes;
- dietary changes to low-fat and low- cholesterol foods;
- weight reduction;
- incorporating exercise into his or her daily lifestyle;
- smoking cessation.

Cardiac rehabilitation nurses are typically employed by healthcare facilities and clinics.

Self-employment ideas include:
* consulting;
* teaching;
* providing staff to cardiac rehab units in healthcare facilities;
* presenting seminars and courses for the public on life-style changes and smoking cessation;
* operating fixed or mobile cardiac rehab facilities owned and operated by nurses providing cardiac rehabilitation to urban and rural areas;
* operating fitness centers owned and operated by nurses that include cardiac rehabilitation;
* offering products, such as multimedia audio and video presentations and books teaching lifestyle changes, weight reduction, exercise, and wellness.

Case Management

Case management nurses work with patients of all ages and diagnoses. However, most specialize in areas of HIV/AIDS, rehabilitation, and geriatrics. The goal is to maximize health and minimize cost by utilizing the proper treatment at the proper time while maintaining continuity and quality care. The nurse coordinates the care provided by the physician and other healthcare workers.

Case management nurses are knowledgeable in both the clinical and financial aspects of healthcare. Case managers are typically employed by healthcare facilities as well as the health maintenance organizations, and the insurance industry. The services of consultants are needed in healthcare facilities and in the insurance industry as large corporations downsize and terminate in-house positions.

Self-employment ideas include:
- consulting;
- teaching;
- medical underwriting;
- designing and writing patient pathways;
- operating an agency providing managed care nurses to healthcare facilities, managed care organizations, and insurance companies.

Education and Training

Nurse educators are responsible for educating student nurses and providing continuing education and training for practicing nurses. The level of education required depends on the educational setting.

Nurse educators are often clinical specialists with advance degrees. However, more and more practicing nurses want continuing education from nurses who have current experience at the bedside. Current practice experience can be more important than advanced degrees to some nurses looking for continuing education.

Nurse educators are typically employed by schools of nursing and healthcare facilities to provide education to staff members.

Self-employment ideas include:
- consulting;
- teaching;
- designing and selling multimedia educational products including books and seminars;
- offering CPR, ACLS, PALS instruction and certification, and certification review classes;

- presenting review classes for certification in all nursing specialties offering certification.

Emergency Medical Services Pre-hospital

The emergency medical pre-hospital nurse works with patients of all ages and diagnoses who need emergency, pre-hospital treatment at the scene, and/or transport.

Pre-hospital emergency nurses are typically employed by pre-hospital emergency medical services; healthcare facilities, and high-risk transport services.

Self-employment ideas include:

- consulting;
- teaching;
- operating air and surface ambulance transport services;
- developing and operating teaching institutes that teach emergency medical technicians, paramedics, and 911 dispatchers;
- presenting classes for certification in ACLS, CPR, and PALS;
- operating businesses that provide medical personnel on ships and classes to certify the ship's personnel in life support;
- operating companies that train and certify individuals in life support and sell automated external defibrillators for other companies;
- providing nursing staff on cruises.

Emergency Nursing

The emergency nurse cares for patients of all ages and diagnoses who need emergency care in an acute care facility in an emergency department or trauma unit.

are provided includes critical and non-critical care. Emergency nurses are able to respond quickly and appropriately to stabilize patients and make critical decisions independently.

Emergency nurses are typically employed by healthcare facilities, teaching institutions that train emergency medical service personnel, cruise lines, camps, and resorts.

Self-employment ideas include:

- consulting and teaching;
- training and certification for ACLS, CPR, and PALS;
- teaching and mentoring emergency medical technicians and paramedics;
- writing and teaching continuing education for emergency nurses;
- multimedia educational presentations;
- writing core curriculum;
- writing continuing education;
- emergency management consulting;
- sales and after-the-sale programs for automatic external defibrillators (AED);
- presenting seminars for emergency nurses to teach the knowledge base needed to become certified.

Forensic Nursing

Forensic nurses work in areas of nursing that interact with the law. The following are the eight practice areas of forensic nursing.

- interpersonal violence
- emergency and trauma
- patient care facilities issues

- forensic mental health
- public health and safety
- correctional nursing
- death investigation
- legal nurse consulting

Forensic nursing science is an investigative approach. It explains the events and associated medical-legal issues that result in the aftermath of these events when injury is sustained by trauma, abuse, neglect, violence, traumatic accidents, and traumatic events of nature. A clinical forensic nurse provides care to both the victim and the perpetrator and defends the patients' legal rights through the collection and documentation of forensic evidence. The goal of a forensic nurse is to competently and objectively collect, document, photograph, contain, and preserve evidence. A forensic nurse seeks the truth through an investigative approach and testifies to their findings without bias.

Forensic nurses are typically employed by healthcare facilities, law enforcement agencies, correctional facilities, coroner's offices, medical examiner's offices, and insurance companies.

Self-employment ideas include:

- consulting;
- teaching;
- operating private autopsy facilities;
- acting as deputy coroner;
- offering private investigative services;
- providing correction nurses to staff prison facilities;
- providing nurse examiners to law enforcement agencies;

- owner-operator of free standing facilities.

Genetic Nursing

Genetic nurses care for people's genetic health including screening for early detection, risk identification, and treatment. They care for patients of all ages with acute or chronic genetic illnesses. Care includes advocacy, teaching, counseling, case management, and research.

Genetic nurses are typically employed by healthcare facilities, universities, and research facilities.

Self-employment ideas include:

- consulting;
- teaching;
- lobbying;
- collecting and analyzing data;
- writing grants.

Holistic Nursing

Holistic nurses treat patients of all ages with acute or chronic illnesses or injuries on an outpatient basis. Care includes treating the whole person not just the disease. Holistic practitioners include massage therapists, acupuncturists, and general holistic nurses. These nurses focus on wellness from a spiritual and natural perspective.

Holistic nurses are typically employed by healthcare facilities, holistic clinics, spas, pain management centers, health clubs, and holistic resorts.

Self-employment ideas include:

- consulting;
- teaching;

- operating a holistic bed and breakfast resort, fitness club, or health club;
- practicing independently;
- presenting multimedia presentations;
- selling products;
- teaching holistic treatment modalities to the public;
- operating a seminar business.

Infection Control Nursing

Infection control nurses identify, track, and control infections in healthcare facilities, develop methods of prevention in healthcare facilities, implement immunization programs, and develop biological terrorist response protocols. No patient care is involved.

Infection control nurses are typically employed by healthcare facilities.

Self-employment ideas include:

- consulting;
- teaching;
- performing pre- and post-regulatory survey consultations;
- offering consultations on nosocomial infection eradication and prevention;
- writing policy and procedure for healthcare facilities;
- writing guidelines for organizations and facilities;
- writing mandates for regulatory organizations and governmental agencies.

Informatics Nursing

Nurse informaticists work with computerized data

and the hardware required for collecting the data. Nursing informatics is a combination of nursing and computer science. It involves no patient care.

Data analysis is used throughout healthcare to reduce risk and improve quality of care. The goal of informatics is to improve efficiency, reduce risk, and improve patient care.

Specialization includes:

- data analysis;
- systems management;
- software design;
- training;
- systems installation;
- sales;
- market planning.

Informatic nurses typically are employed by healthcare facilities, computer hardware and software companies, educational institutions, regulatory agencies, pharmaceutical and research companies, and medical libraries.

Self-employment ideas include:

- consulting;
- teaching;
- designing documentation systems;
- designing management systems;
- training;
- providing data analysis;
- developing and selling software and hardware including manufacturing.

Intravenous Nursing

Intravenous nurses treat patients of all ages with acute or chronic illnesses or injuries who require intravenous therapy. Care includes accessing the intravenous site, providing medications, blood, fluids, and nutrition including initiating, monitoring, and terminating therapy.

Intravenous nurses are typically employed by healthcare facilities, clinics, and home care agencies. Self-employment ideas include:

- consulting;
- teaching;
- owning and operating clinics for intravenous therapy;
- staffing agencies for acute and long-term facilities with intravenous nurses on a need-for-service basis;
- inserting intravenous lines for other nurses to manage fluids and medication;
- providing education to practicing nurses on intravenous insertion techniques and management of intravenous fluids, medications, and nutrition.

Legal Field: Non-lawyer Professionals

The legal field uses physicians and other healthcare professionals to determine the healthcare issues in a law suit.

Nurses entered this role in the mid-1970s in cases that involved workers' compensation and rehabilitation. At that time, the plan of the insurance companies and defense was to decrease the disability and therefore, decrease the financial settlement. Legal nurse consulting (described below) is but one of the areas of practice.

The registered nurse is now an active player of the healthcare professionals (social workers, physical therapists, occupational therapists, vocational rehabilitation counselors.)

Legal nurses are typically employed by law firms and insurance companies.

Some of the major players are listed below.

- Legal nurse consultants evaluate, analyze, and render an informed opinion on the delivery of healthcare and the resulting outcomes. More details are under the specialty later in this book.

- Life care planners formulate a care plan for the life of the patient using financial codes to determine future money needed to care for the claimant's disability.

- Rehabilitation nurses work towards getting the client as well as possible and ultimately reduce the amount of money needed to care for the client's healthcare needs related to the disability.

- Workers' compensation nurses work towards getting the client back to work and managing his healthcare to decrease the disability and increase the client's function.

- Elder care managers work with the elderly to see they are provided with services that help them age in place or move them to an appropriate lifestyle and protect them against fraud.

These nurses often work for elder trust attorneys and for families who do not live near the patient.

- Case managers work towards getting the clients to needed services within their network.

- Nurse paralegals work with an attorney and offer legal services as well as working with healthcare issues.

- Medicare Set-Aside consultants write a financial document forecasting the medical needs of the client throughout life. Economists take the medical needs and project them into the future. These plans are used to determine settlement amounts and to set-aside funds to use after they receive Medicare. Medicare requires that the responsible party set-aside funds for future care.

- Forensic nurses collect and preserve evidence from the victim and the documentation.

Business and self-employment opportunities include:

- consulting service;

- staffing service providing these consultants to law firms and insurance companies.

Legal Nurse Consulting

The American Association of Legal Nurse Consultants states, "The primary role of the legal nurse consultant is to evaluate, analyze, and render informed opinions on the delivery of health care and the resulting outcomes."

The association lists the services that a legal nurse

consultant provides to include:

- identifying standards of care, causation, and damage issues;
- conducting client interviews;
- conducting research and summarizing medical literature;
- applying multidisciplinary standards of care and regulatory requirements;
- preparing chronologies of medical events and comparing and correlating them to the allegations;
- educating attorneys regarding medical facts and issues relevant to the case;
- identifying and determining damages and related costs of services, including collaborating with economists in preparing a cost analysis for damages;
- assisting with depositions and trials, including developing and preparing exhibits;
- organizing medical records and other medically related litigation materials;
- locating and procuring demonstrative evidence;
- collaborating with attorneys in preparing or analyzing complaints, answers, and motions for summary judgment, interrogatories, deposition and trial outlines, queries for direct and cross examination, document production requests, trial briefs, demand letters, and status reports
- identifying and retaining expert witnesses;
- acting as a liaison among attorneys, physicians, and clients;
- providing initial case screening for merit

Areas of practice include:

- personal injury;
- product liability;
- medical negligence;
- toxic torts;
- workers' compensation;
- risk management;
- medical licensure investigation;
- fraud and abuse;
- compliance;
- criminal law;
- elder law;
- other applicable cases.

Legal nurse consultants are typically employed by healthcare facilities in risk management, with insurance companies, and plaintiff and defense legal firms.

Self-employment ideas include:
- consulting;
- teaching;
- operating an agency providing legal nurse consultants to attorneys on a need-for-service basis;
- writing continuing education for legal nurses;
- writing textbooks for legal nurses;
- designing and operating institutes to teach legal nurse consulting;
- presenting seminars for legal nurses.

Labor and Delivery

Obstetrical nurses care for mothers and babies at the time of delivery and teach mothers to care for and feed their infants. Breastfeeding is learned and not instinctual for today's woman. New mothers need proper evaluation and education.

Labor and delivery nurses are typically employed by healthcare facilities and birthing clinics.

Self-employment ideas include:

- offering breast pump rentals, sales, and service;
- providing home visits and education for mothers and families;
- providing lactation consulting services.

International Board Certified Lactation Consultants (IBCLCs) are healthcare providers working towards assisting families in making informed choices regarding their infant feeding practices. The clinical practice of the IBCLC lactation consultant focuses on providing lactation care and clinical management.

This is accomplished through collaboration with other members of the health care team and the client. IBCLC lactation consultants are responsible for decisions and actions undertaken as a part of their professional role in the management of lactation or breastfeeding issues, including:

- assessment, planning, intervention, and evaluation of care in a variety of situations;
- prevention of problems;
- complete, accurate, and timely documentation of care;
- communication and collaboration with other health care professionals including:
  - assessment information
  - suggested interventions
  - instructions provided

Nephrology Nursing

Nephrology nurses care for patients of all ages with renal dysfunction. They focus on the physical and psychological aspects of kidney dysfunction while implementing treatment modalities including hemodialysis, peritoneal dialysis, and care of the kidney transplant patient.

Nephrology nurses typically are employed by healthcare facilities, renal dialysis centers and clinics, and home health agencies.

Self-employment ideas include:

- consulting;
- teaching;
- operating a fixed and/or mobile dialysis unit;
- providing nephrology nurses to dialysis units and healthcare facilities;
- presenting nursing continuing education seminars and certification review courses;
- designing and providing public wellness programs and support groups.

Parish Nursing

The parish nurse treats patients of all ages with acute or chronic illnesses or injuries on an outpatient basis. Parish nursing brings together healthcare, community, and the church.

Services provided include:

- education;
- healthcare counseling;

- bereavement counseling;
- program design and presentation;
- resource nurse and liaison between healthcare and religions that limit healthcare options.

Parish nurses are typically full or part-time volunteers with religious organizations and congregations.

Self-employment ideas include:

- consulting;
- teaching;
- providing nonprofit organizations with nurses to staff missionary outposts.

Pediatric Nursing

Pediatric nurses treat children and their families in a variety of settings. The patient age group is from newborn to adolescence. The patients are seen in healthcare inpatient and outpatient facilities, clinics, and home care.

Care and services include all aspects of physical and psychosocial nursing care.

- patient and family education
- case management
- discharge planning to restore, maintain or promote the physical and psychological health of children and adolescents

Pediatric nurses are typically employed by healthcare facilities (hospitals, clinics, daycare centers, and camps) and home care agencies.

Self-employment ideas include:

- consulting;
- teaching;

- providing pediatric nurses to staff healthcare facilities and home health agencies.

Pharmaceutical and Medical Sales

Nurse salespersons sell and promote pharmaceutical and medical products and services. Selling often involves exhibiting at trade shows, travel to facilities purchasing the products, and educating and training the customer after the sale.

Nurse salespersons are typically employed by pharmaceutical and medical products companies as well as direct marketing firms.

Self-employment ideas include:

- consulting;
- teaching;
- inventing a medical service or product;
- designing a medical service or product;
- manufacturing a medical service or product
- selling a medical service or product;
- writing Federal Drug Administration documentation.

Recruiter

The nurse recruiter brings nurses to the employment arena for healthcare facilities by direct contact, trade shows, and even travel to foreign countries for nurse recruitment. No patient contact is involved.

Nurse recruiters are typically employed by healthcare facilities.

Self-employment ideas include:

- consulting;
- teaching;

- operating nurse and healthcare personnel brokerages;
- operating recruiting companies;
- operating placement companies that recruit from foreign countries.

Rehabilitation Nursing

The rehabilitation nurse cares for patients with temporary or permanent disabilities. Care includes triage, patient education, pain management, case management, and discharge planning to restore, maintain, or promote return to maximum function.

Rehabilitation nurses are typically employed by healthcare facilities, rehabilitation centers, and long-term and acute skilled care facilities.

Self-employment ideas include:

- consulting;
- teaching;
- staffing agencies specializing in rehabilitation nurses for rehabilitation centers;
- operating inpatient assisted care and skilled nursing facilities;
- operating daycare centers;
- operating home care agencies.

Research Nursing

Research nurses work with all aspects of pharmaceutical, nursing, and medical research. Patient care can be involved when working with clinical research centers that monitor patients.

Research nurses are typically employed by pharmaceutical companies, research centers and universities, clinics, and healthcare facilities.

Self-employment ideas include:

- consulting;
- teaching;
- writing grants;
- analyzing data.

Senior Health Services

Registered nurses care for older adults and provide a wide variety of services.

Senor health nurses are typically employed by healthcare facilities providing services to seniors and senior centers.

Self-employment ideas are diverse and may include:

- consulting;
- teaching;
- providing foot care services;
- providing medication management, counseling, and supervision;
- offering home safety assessments and supplying recommendations;
- providing private duty nursing services;
- offering case management;
- offering care management services.

Travel Nursing

The travel nurse cares for patients of all ages. They supplement staff in healthcare facilities. A travel nurse often specializes and only works in his or her area of expertise. Care provided by a travel nurse includes all aspects of patient care in a variety of specialty areas.

Travel nurses are typically employed by temporary

healthcare staffing agencies.

Self-employment ideas include;

- consulting;
- teaching;
- operating staffing agencies providing travel nurses to healthcare facilities.

Conclusion

This chapter describes the specialties of nursing. Based on this information, it can be concluded that self-employment options occur in all specialties.

Chapter 8
Roadblocks

Roadblocks are imagined obstacles that prevent or delay individuals from becoming entrepreneurs. They are part of the individual's mindset and not actual physical barriers. Certain roadblocks are unique to nurses and are developed over years of working as a nurse in a healthcare facility.

These roadblocks are thought to develop because nurses are responsible for the patient's life and by being under the control of physicians and hospital administration. These roadblocks can cause anxiety and fear that lead to procrastination. Some of the major roadblocks are defined as follows.

Big Business Roadblock

Thinking that becoming an entrepreneur means moving directly from staff nurse to an owner-operator of a big business can be a roadblock to starting a business. The fear is real and justified. No one can successfully move from being an employee to an owner of a big business in one leap. More knowledge about business is needed to recognize that businesses are started small and built one step at a time. When nurses learn the steps to building a small business, the fear subsides and the transition can be made more easily.

Instant Response Roadblock

Thinking that you will see an instant response when you start a business can be a roadblock. Nurses get used to seeing rapid responses, like popping a nitro and the chest pain is gone or giving a bolus of diuretic and the patient breathes easily. Kathy Shea, R.N., of Seattle likens a small business to counseling a 450-pound patient back to a healthy weight of 150. It takes time. You need to move slowly and be consistently vigilant and flexible in your approach. Being a business owner resembles long-term care.

I Can Do It Myself Roadblock

The National Nurses in Business Association, Inc. (NNBA) provides support for the business element and bridges the gap between nursing and business. The NNBA provides information on RN self-employment opportunities, offers business education, acts as a national voice, and maintains a national networking arena.

Specialty associations, such as the American Association of Legal Nurse Consultants, The American Association of Nurse Attorneys, American Association of Holistic Nurses, and American Academy of Nurse Practitioners, provide specific knowledge related to the service provided. Thinking you can do it by yourself can slow your progress. Nurse businesses have two distinctive and separate elements—the nursing and the business. A strong support system for both elements is essential.

The Small Business Development Center (SBDC) a division of the Small Business Administration is available to offer local business support. Unfortunately, nurses often relate their business ideas in medical lingo and do not communicate well with the business community.

For example, a nursing agency is called a temporary help service in the business community. Consulting is a broad classification that includes teaching, offering continuing education, training, public speaking, writing, seminars, workshops, legal nurse consulting, and being an expert witness, among others. Contracting your nursing services to patients is independent contracting. The SBDC can help you set up a temporary help service, a consultancy, or an independent contracting business. The basic business foundation is the same regardless of the type of staff, the type of consulting, or the type of independent contracting.

Feeling Unworthy Roadblock

Thinking you are unworthy is a roadblock. The career of nursing is perceived as requiring creativity, providing independence, and offering a variety of work options. It attracts creative, independent, and option-oriented people. Unfortunately, nursing is traditionally a profession in which nurses must take orders and follow procedures, standards, and clinical pathways. A nurse's self-worth suffers as he or she is asked to perform repetitive tasks and is penalized for creativity and choosing options other than the written procedures. This mismatch leads to burnout, dissatisfaction, and feelings of low self-esteem.

Nurses are exposed to physicians and hospital administrative personnel who constantly remind them of their lowly positions on the healthcare team. The wide differences in income and social status are other reminders of the nurse's lower position of worth. Often nurses have a hard time establishing a fee for their services because they do not know the worth of their services.

Once you become aware that you may be suffering from a feeling of low self-esteem, you can develop a plan to remedy that. As a nurse, you are highly skilled, possess all the skills listed in a past issue of the *Occupation Outlook Handbook* published by the U.S. Department of Labor, are college educated, highly knowledgeable in medical and supportive fields, and possess a great artistic talent—the art of nursing. As a nurse, you are worthy!

I Don't Know How to Start a Business Roadblock

Thinking there is no more to learn about nursing can prevent you from learning about nurse entrepreneurship. Just because it was not taught in nursing school doesn't mean it is not a vital part of nursing. This roadblock can easily be overcome by learning about business startup.

Desire for Perfection Roadblock

Thinking everything needs to be perfect and we need to have all our ducks in a row before beginning delays startup. As nurses, we are taught that one deviation from perfection can mean a patient's life and that we must have all our ducks in a row. Once we recognize we are striving for perfection and realize that we don't have to be perfect to start a business, we can get on with the business of starting the business.

There is no perfect business name, no perfect location, and no perfect type of business entity. When we strive for perfection in everything we do, we miss opportunities that arise while we are striving for that elusive perfection.

Roadblock Breakers

The journey from employee to entrepreneur is filled with roadblocks. Once the roadblock is recognized, a plan can be developed to overcome that barrier, and we can continue toward the rewards of entrepreneurship—a higher income, independence, and respect.

Nurse entrepreneur Sandra Ernat, RN RNC MS CNAA, president of Health and Safety International, Inc. and Ernat and Associates Consulting Services, Ltd. of LaSalle, Illinois, writes, "Looking back, fear was my obstacle to starting my own nursing business full-time. I had been a legal nurse consultant for many years on a part-time basis. But this was different than actually incorporating two businesses and going full time."

"I read books, like *Feel the Fear and Do it Anyway*! Talking with my peers was not helpful because they did not understand why I would want to work for myself and give up the security of a job. I educated myself on the business aspects by reading everything I could, contacting the Small Business Administration and the Small Business Development Center on the campus of our local community college."

"The business tools I gathered from my research are transferable to a nursing business. I knew that I could run my own business. I would recall frequently something I had read many years ago, 'If you keep doing what you've always done, you'll keep getting what you've always got.' If you're serious about starting your own business, you have to break out of your comfort zone and JUST DO IT!!! Remember, if you have a choice between freedom and security, and you choose security—you have neither."

Colleen Lindell, RN MHSA CNOR CLNC, president of Med-Legal.net, Inc. of Osceola, Wisconsin relates, "The one and only obstacle that delayed me from starting my own business was in my mind. A voice inside me was saying, 'How do you know how to be successful? You've never gone out on your own before. What makes you think you have what it takes? What if you don't have what it takes or you really don't like being your own boss? It's risky business. Are you willing to put your family and your family's income on the line so that I can be a business owner? Isn't that a bit selfish?

"To overcome that mindset, I put forth a surge of positive energy and belief in myself. I reminded myself of past achievements both as a staff nurse and department manager. I thought about how much I enjoyed challenges and the personal satisfaction of being part of a worthwhile task or activity. When I was able to rid myself of the fear of success, personal growth and financial gain resulted. Since I started on my journey from employee to business owner in 1996, my business has annually doubled both in customers and in financial net gain. If you wish to become an entrepreneur, my advice to you is to consider your strengths, weaknesses, opportunities, and threats. Focus in on your strengths to overcome weaknesses and pursue opportunities that eliminate or reduce threats to your business. Additionally, eliminate what can be your worst enemy—your own mindset! Believe in yourself and focus on creating and maintaining positive energy in all that you do."

Cindy Banes, RN, LNCC, a nurse entrepreneur from St. Louis, Missouri, writes, "Nursing has traditionally been a profession in which nurses take orders and are not comfortable asking for what they want and need. A paradigm shift needs to occur for nurses to truly recognize and appreciate all the valuable assets nurses have and can bring to the table in the world of business. Often seen as stumbling blocks, the obstacles of, 'but I don't have...,' can very easily be turned into stepping stones up a staircase to success. By changing your mindset to one of abundance versus one of scarcity, one can achieve dramatic growth."

The rewards of nurse entrepreneurship are professional satisfaction, respect, independence, and the opportunity to create a higher income. By learning more about roadblocks, nurses can identify and eliminate their personal roadblocks, begin the journey from employee to entrepreneur, and reap the rewards.

Chapter 9
Business Lingo

The business community communicates in business lingo. Nurses communicate in medical lingo. When a nurse talks with the business community, there may be a problem exchanging information. Learning the business terms is part of the preparation needed to start a business.

It's your responsibility to learn the business language. After all, you are entering the business arena. Business professionals, such as insurance agents, real estate agents, loan officers, attorneys, accountants, and tax preparers, are often confused when the words nurse or nursing are included in the business description.

NAICS

When describing your business, it is best to use the North American Classification System (NAICS). It is the standard nomenclature for business establishments in the U.S. Each business is assigned a numeric code. For example, what a nurse would call a nursing agency is a temporary staffing service in business terms.

These numeric codes for industry were started in the early 1900s and evolved into the Standard Industry Classification (SIC) of 1987. The SIC was the official numeric codes classification for all businesses in the U.S. until 1997, when the statistical agencies of the United States, Canada, and Mexico joined together to develop a comprehensive system to classify industry in all of North America. These North American Identification Codes (NAIC) assigned to industries by the United States Department of Commerce have replaced the SIC. New codes have been added for new industries spawned by the Internet and the recent information explosion.

The NAIC classifications are used to gather industry data and develop statistics. The statistics are used to look at the history of an industry and project future trends.

The NAIC code is used on business tax returns. State and federal governments compare similar businesses to each other to determine the average expenses and incomes within an industry. When one company is out of line with other similar businesses in the same industry, a tax audit often follows.

The business community does not know what a nurse does and often minimizes nursing to what is seen on television and in the movies. The fact that you are a nurse often muddies the communication between the business community and a nurse entrepreneur.

Nurse practitioners who practice nursing are classified as 621399: Offices of All Other Miscellaneous Health Practitioners. This U.S. industry comprises establishments of independent health practitioners (except physicians; dentists; chiropractors; optometrists; mental health specialists; physical, occupational, and speech therapists; audiologists; and podiatrists). These practitioners operate private or group practices in their own offices (e.g., centers, clinics) or in the facilities of others, such as hospitals or HMO medical centers.

Temporary staffing services (nursing or staffing agencies) are classified as 561320: Temporary Help Services. This industry comprises establishments primarily engaged in supplying workers to clients' businesses for limited periods of time to supplement the working force of the client. The individuals provided are employees of the temporary help service establishment.

Worker Status

To further complicate the issue, two worker statuses exist in the U.S. designated by the Internal Revenue Service (IRS). One is employee and the other is independent contractor. These terms have a legal definition to describe methods used to pay taxes. The employee's taxes are withheld from the employees pay by the employer and sent to the IRS. The employer does not withhold the independent contractor's taxes.

The IRS has the final word on worker status for tax purposes. Some nursing agencies hire nurses as independent contractors when they should be hiring them as employees. The contract between agencies and nurses often include a clause that states the nurse (worker) will be responsible for any back employee taxes and penalties if the IRS determines that the nurse (worker) is employee status and not independent contactor status.

If you have a question regarding your worker status as an independent contractor, ask the IRS by completing the IRS form SS8 (Determination of Worker Status for Purposes of Federal Employment Taxes and Income Tax Withholding) available at www.IRS.gov.

Business Concept

When you begin to formulate your business idea, use business terms. An idea becomes a business concept when it has four crucial parts as follows.

1. A product or service you are offering for sale

2. A customer who will buy your product or service and pay you for it

3. A value proposition, a benefit the customer sees in the product or service

4. A way to get the product or service to the customer

Ask yourself what business you are in and don't make your vision too narrow. The best example of being too narrow is about a railroad company that limited their vision to the business of trains and tracks. When trains were replaced with trucks and highways, the railroad company was left behind. Had their business vision been transporting goods and people, new methods of travel would have expanded their business and not limited it.

Your business description is a broad vision of what business you are in. This business description becomes part of your business plan.

How to Become a Self-Employed RN and/or Business Owner

Easy Business Description Process:

Use the following three-step process to develop your business description.

1. Start the description with whether you are a product or service business.
2. For the next few words or word, use an action, process, or art, such as transporting, educating, expanding, promoting, teaching, writing, lobbying, etc.
3. Next use a noun to which the action refers, such as transporting goods or people; educating registered nurses; expanding business knowledge of nurse entrepreneurs; promoting sports events; teaching children or patients; writing nursing education, or lobbying for or against a specific cause.

The following are examples of business descriptions.

- A product retail business making and selling handmade crafts

- A product wholesale business making, distributing, and supplying homemade crafts

- A service business providing nursing services

- A service business educating nurses

The business world is not going to take time to learn nursing or medical lingo. To communicate with the business world, you must learn to speak in their terms.

When meeting with a businessperson, at times, it is to your advantage to refer to yourself as a healthcare professional and not a nurse. The picture of a nurse giving bedpans and pills is very much a part of the

U.S. culture. Working with business professionals to learn their lingo and terms makes starting a business much easier.

Part II: How to Start the Business

Chapter 10
Names and Logos

Business Name

What is in a business name? Everything! The wrong name can prevent your business from growing and keep it in the shadows. A great name can bring your business into the light and help it grow and become successful.

Business names are not about creativity but rather about marketing. Often a name cannot be chosen until after the business description and goals are determined. Naming the business is not always the first step. When you are ready to name the business, start by deciding what you want your business name to communicate.

Your name can communicate a statement about your business regarding:

- quality;
- value;
- expertise;

- respect;
- the distinctiveness of your product or service;
- the key elements of your business.

There is a lot of debate about what makes a name for a business. Names can be abstract leaving the consumer to create the image. Names can be informative and create the image immediately in the mind of the consumer. Names can be coined or made-up and not even be real words.

The name Acura of Honda Motor Co. has no particular meaning but suggests precision. Professional naming firms start with up to a thousand names and work from there; rejecting names that are already in use or registered and finally coming up with what they think is ideal.

There are many resources for business naming, ranging from the free advice of a friend, relative, or online at governmental and private sites; instant name-generating computer programs costing $19.95 to professional business naming firms that cost from hundreds to thousands of dollars.

The final name should best define your company's objectives, accurately describe what company you have in mind, and be a name you like.

Dos and don'ts for business names

Dos	Don'ts
Do choose a name that appeals to customers not just you.	Don't use a name that only appeals to you.
Do choose a name that is short, easy to spell, and pronounce.	Don't choose a name that has multiple spellings, is hard for a third grader to spell, and can be misheard, e.g., the letters S versus the letter F.
Do choose a name that gets customers to respond on an emotional level.	Don't choose a name that is unemotional or not moving.
Do choose a name that is comfortable, familiar, and brings to mind pleasing memories for the customer.	Don't pick a name that causes embarrassment or unpleasant memories.
Do choose a name that is short and to the point.	Don't pick a name that is long or confusing or embarrassing.
Do choose a name that is available as a .com domain name.	Don't choose a name that is not available as a .com domain name.
Do register the domain name.	Don't wait to register the domain name.

Dos	Don'ts
Do choose a name that is understandable in our multicultural society.	Don't pick a name that you consider cute or witty. It can be easily misunderstood.
Use the specific legal designation for your business structure.	Don't use Inc. as part of your name unless your company is actually incorporated.
Do use specific descriptions for others in your business, e.g., & Sons, Associates, Partners	Don't use the word Enterprises. Today it has the mark of an amateur.
Do use words in your business name that have broad definitions.	Don't use geographical locations. Don't use specific names. They can limit your growth.
Use your own name if possible, for example Bemis Consulting. The website would be www.bemisconsulting.com Customers are often looking for a person.	Don't use first names. They sound homemade and nonprofessional. Good for a local bakeshop, but not for a professional consulting or staffing service.

Logos

A logo is a symbol designed for easy and definite

recognition of your company. Your logo is a graphical expression of you and your company. It is your brand.

Branding is not new and can be traced back some 4,000 years to the ancient Egyptians. Cave inscriptions and writings indicate that cattle were branded as early as 2,000 BC. It was an effective way of marking ownership of animals and people.

In the U.S., cattle brands identified the owner of the ranch, and stood for the owner's reputation of honor, quality, and fair dealings. Cowboy often rode for the brand never knowing the owner. Cowboys' reputations were identified with the brand they rode for. The reputation of honesty—providing a quality product and dealing fairly—was sought after then and is still sought after today. Many business employees do not know the owners of the business, but they remain loyal to the company because of the reputation that is presented by the brand.

Businesses used the concept of the cowboy brands and designed logos (brands) in colored geometric shapes, such as circles and squares often combined with letters, e.g., the Nike® checkmark or swoosh; the Harley Davidson® geometric shape that includes their name (often used as a tattoo by their devoted customers); Toyota's® circle and sphere shape; and Honda's® H in a rounded rectangle for cars and the wing over the name Honda for the motorcycles. Brands are not carved in stone and can be redesigned or changed as the business evolves and business trends change.

These geometric shapes can easily be placed on a marketing piece whether it is letterhead, brochure, cloth tee shirt, or tote bag. The logo can be placed on any type of media. Large complex images and photographs as logos do not lend themselves to the quick identification like a simple geometrical shape, and most importantly, don't lend themselves to printing. Learn from the big boys and keep your logo geometric and simple. The fee for graphic design services for a logo ranges from free to several thousands dollars.

I recommend that you take your basic 8-color crayon set and start doodling. When you have something you like, ask (or hire) a graphic artist to turn it into graphic art. Many software programs are available and you probably can do it yourself. It doesn't need any hidden meaning. It is just a brand, a means of graphically identifying your business.

What's your brand?

Chapter 11
Advertising

Advertising is a method used to call public attention to your business. It emphasizes the desirable qualities of your products and services to produce a desire to patronize your business. Advertisements are not limited to magazine and Internet ads. Advertisements include business cards, brochures and other printed documents, web pages, and tip sheets.

Most likely, you are not knowledgeable about or experienced in writing advertising. Since you know more about your business than anyone else, the following tips will help you write effective advertisements.

Style

A business style is made up of colors, images, and words and should clearly represent the service or product the business is offering. Your style should mirror your client. For example, if your clientele are attorneys use a legal style, if your clientele works with children, use a child-like style.

Printed documents and website pages for your business should use the same style as used on business cards and brochures.

Language

Advertising language should not include big words, flowery language, or slang and professional lingo. Potential customers will throw the advertisement in the trash before they will look up a word in a dictionary.

Write Advertising to Get Your Message Out

In order to be effective, advertising must be read or heard by your potential customers. They must consider it and make a decision to purchase your product or service.

Customers only read or listen to customer-centered advertisements or public announcements. All the while, the customer is thinking, "What's in it for me?" Unless the customer sees or hears what's in it for them, the advertisement doesn't even enter his or her conscious mind. Advertisements and public announcements that refer to what the customer wants are called customer-centered.

Businesspersons often talk about and agonize over what their customers want. So the businesspersons do surveys, but surveys generally do not show the customers' viewpoints. Instead, they only put the businesses' ideas into the mind of the customers. In order to find out what the customers want, you must ask the customers what they want from your business.

Don't ask customers what they want just one time. Ask customers what they want at every contact. Ask customers if there is any other product or service they want or need. Ask customers at every contact if they have any suggestion or tips on how to improve the business's service or product to better meet their needs. Write down the answers in front of the customer so that the customer feels that their suggestions have importance.

The time to ask questions is when the customer receives a service or product. Be subtle with your questions. Only ask them if they fit into the conversation. With a little experience, you can gather information regarding what a customer wants with every customer contact. Letting the customer know that you are considering making a change often promotes an honest opinion from the customer.

- "We are considering some changes. Do you have any suggestions?"

- "If we changed our business hours, what hours would best suit you?"

- "We are considering changing our phone system. How many telephone rings are you comfortable with before a person answers the phone?"

- "We are considering changing our phone system. Do you mind leaving a message?"

Write About Your Customers—Not Your Company.

So many times a businessperson can't wait to write that first brochure. There are so many exciting things to say about the company. Often, these facts are exciting only to the people who represent the business. The customers could care less. Advertising should be customer-centered. Instead of telling all the wonderful things the company can do, write about what the customers will receive. Customers want to know "What's in it for me?" Using the word you is effective when used frequently throughout advertisements.

For example:

- "You don't pay a penny up front."

- "You get more respect."

- "You get service when you want it 24/7."

- "Here is what you need!"

Being Clever or Cute Is Not a Good Idea

An ad headline stating, "We take you over the moon," and an awesome picture of the moon taken from space won't impress customers. Clever or cute advertising can be misinterpreted and cause the business to lose customers instead of gaining them.

Write the Same Way You Talk

Advertising is effective when it can be easily read out loud by a company representative to a customer and convince the customer to buy the product. The written language should be the same as the spoken words used with a customer. Don't use big words when a small word will do.

Jerry Della Femina, a famous copywriter, said, "Nobody has the time to try and figure out what you are trying to say so you need to be direct. Most great advertising is direct. That's how people talk. That's the style they read. That's what sells products, services, and ideas!"

Forget What Your English Teacher Taught You

Nurse Entrepreneur Martha Mitschke offers the following advice in her book *How to Start Your Own $100,000 Nursing Agency.* Forget what your English teacher told you about not starting your sentences with words such as And, Or, So, or But. When you want to keep a person reading, the best thing to do is start your sentences with And, Or, So or But. It connects your ideas and it is the way you speak.

Examples are:

- And you can call....
- Or you can e-mail...
- So you always have someone available...
- But you have other options . . .

Don't Write in Complete Sentences

All sentences don't need a subject and a predicate. Simple sentences with action verbs are the most effective. Some rules of grammar, however, should not be broken. A good book on the subject is *The Elements of Style* by William Strunk and E. B. White, a short 92-page book on grammar and style that can be read in one evening.

Make Yourself Look Good

The two main categories of font styles are san serif (font without feet) and serif (font with feet). San serif is excellent for headlines. Serif is easier to read and better for a body of text. The font used in this book is Century Schoolbook, but there are many other choices. Bold is great for headlines and bold italics can be used for very short subheads. Robin Williams's book the

Non-Designers Design Book: Design and Typographic Principles for the Visual Novice is an excellent resource on which fonts to use for different types of documents.

A laser desktop printer that prints 600 dpi can produce quality advertisements at a minimum cost. Over 600 dpi is not needed except for glossy photos.

Software programs are a major consideration. Microsoft Word®, Adobe Photoshop®, and Adobe InDesign® are the current industry standards.

Commercial printers use portable document format (PDF) files. These files cannot be altered and all the images and fonts are embedded in them. A local printer can provide an immediate proof. The electronic file can be emailed to a commercial printer in another area and the proof returned by email of by mail. Portable document files make life a lot easier.

Writing Tip Sheets for Free Advertising

A tip sheet is a form of advertising. It is not blatant advertising. It provides information that the reader can use frequently. Tip sheets are pinned on bulletin boards and kept on the refrigerator door. The tip sheet will be kept longer than a business card or brochure and should not be limited by time-dated material. You can include a magnet with the tip sheet to attach to the potential customer's refrigerator.

The tip sheet can be printed on 8 ½ by 11 paper and is a list of five to nine items. It gives the reader a piece of confidential, advance, or insider information. The tip sheet shows off the writer's knowledge on a given subject. The title indicates the topic covered.

The tip sheet format is simple and straightforward, clean and bold, and fits easily on one page. The tips are typically numbered and separated by an extra line between each numbered item. The writer's contact information is included with an invitation for the reader to email or call the writer with questions or comments.

The tip sheets can be used as a handout at seminars and meetings. Some institutions discourage brochures or advertising. Often an agreement is presented that states the speaker will not distribute advertising. No questions are raised about distributing a tip sheet. A tip sheet is a valuable advertising tool that is quick, easy, effective, and inexpensive. It is a perfect way to power start a new business.

Chapter 12
Customers and Competitors

You've come up with a great idea for the business and you think you are ready to start the business. Hold on! You're not ready until you identify your customers and competitors and then learn everything you can about them.

Customers

The customer goes by many names, such as consumer, buyer, user, client, patron, purchaser, etc. The terms are often specific to certain industries and geographical regions. Consultants have clients. Computer provider companies have users. Stores have patrons. For our purposes, we will use the word customer to define the person or company that will pay you for your products or services.

To increase your chances of success, you must know the following about your customers:

- Who they are.
- Where they are.

- What their wants are.
- When they will purchase.
- How much they are willing to pay for your services or product.

The U.S. Census Bureau estimated the U.S. population at 311,583,000 on June 11, 2011. One person was born every 8 seconds. One death occurred every 13 seconds. One international migrant entered every 43 seconds. This was a net gain of one person every 13 seconds. The world population was estimated at 6, 925,851,573. Searching out customers one-by-one in this vast world of ours is impossible.

The total population needs to be divided into subdivisions or groups that can be considered potential buyers. These groups of customers are called a niche or a segment of the total population that may be interested in purchasing your product or service.

There is no end to the ways you can divide the market and find your niche. In the past, the total population was divided into groups with the defining characteristics being geographical location, age, income, race or culture, and sex.

Geographical boundaries have been crossed with travel and the Internet. You can get on a plane and be anywhere in a matter of hours. Many students in my courses and classes come from across the country and across the oceans. The dream of living in the Caribbean and working with customers in the interior of the U.S. is very doable.

Age is no longer a reliable characteristic to define market segments. Many nurses fifty-years old and up are starting new businesses instead of retiring. Many people are recycling their life skills. Two nurses of the same age can be at opposite places in their lives, one looking at retirement and travel, and the other looking at a way to prolong their life's work. An obstetrical nurse in North Florida is now a writer and calls herself a recycled teenager. A nurse in New York is starting a new family in midlife.

Many purchases are made on credit and although income is important, purchases may not be dependent on income. Retirement savings are often used to start a new business or hobby. Doing what one wants to do in retirement years often takes precedent over making money. Today's customers are cross-cultural and the difference between the sexes is blurred. So, we have to look at segments of the population in new ways to better identify our potential customers or prospects.

Today's customers are smarter than ever before and are not easily grouped with others. Businesses try to develop a niche or special group of people who need or want a product or service. You can use generational groups, cohort groups and life stage groups when identifying your niche group.

Generational Customer Group

A generational customer group is a group of generally contemporaneous individuals regarded as having common cultural or social characteristics and attitudes. An example would be when there is a common period of sequential technological development and innovation, such as the television generation or the computer generation. Baby boomers are doing the same thing now as they did in their thirties; don't make the mistake by grouping them in with seniors. Grandparents, parents, and children can also divide generational groups.

Cohort Customer Group

A cohort customer group defines people by similar life experiences rather than by age or generation. These people form a bond and behave differently than others even of the same age due to common experiences. For example, the veterans of the Vietnam War have different experiences and behave similar to others in their group and different than those of similar age and sex who are not veterans. People who were in college during the late sixties and early 1970s had experiences that were very different from those attending college before and after those years.

Life Stage Customer Group

A life stage customer group defines people in a life stage group who are in the process of doing something, for example getting married, having children, or retiring. This type of group also includes people who are suffering from physical limitations linked to age, such nearsightedness, arthritis, or menopause.

Nichecraft

Lynda C. Falkenstein, author of *Nichecraft, Using Your Specialness to Focus your Business, Corner Your Market and Make Customers Seek You Out*, cautions that you cannot do business with everyone and to keep your niches small and realistic.

Clarify what you are selling.

- I am selling newborn CPR training videos to pregnant women.

- I am selling medical case review services to

plaintiff attorneys.

- I am selling nurse temporary staffing services to acute care hospitals with 50 to 150 inpatient beds.

- I am selling business education seminars to registered nurses considering self-employment.

Describe the customer's viewpoint—look at what you sell from your customer's point of view.

- The pregnant woman is looking for a method to save the baby's life if needed.

- The attorney is looking for cost-effective, time-effective, medical case review from a knowledgeable person.

Test your product and service ideas.

- Talk to your potential customers.

- Give samples.

- Take surveys.

Continue to fine tune the definition of your customer as the business grows. Enter the market when you feel you have minimized the risk.

Reaching Your Customer

Once you have identified your customer niche, you need to reach those customers to tell them your product or services are available.

- Where do they live?

  o You can do a direct mailing.

  o You can include your advertisement with

other mailings.

- Where do they shop?

    o You can put notices on bulletin boards.

    o You can pass out brochures. Ask permission. Some shops don't permit soliciting.

    o You can ask the shop to sell your products.

- To what associations do they belong?

    o You can buy mailing lists from associations.

    o You can advertise your product or service in their trade magazines.

    o You can write articles for their trade magazines.

    o You can sell your products through their catalog. They typically buy at 55% discount and you pay the shipping. They sell the product at retail.

- What magazines do they read?

    o You can place an ad in the magazine.

    o You can write an article for the magazine.

    o Magazines are always looking for other profit centers. Some specialty magazines may purchase your product at a discount and resell it at retail.

    o You can purchase a mailing list of all the people who subscribe to the magazine.

- What radio shows do they listen to?

    o You can have a 30 to 60 second radio advertisement. The cost is about $10 each.

- o   You can be interviewed on talk shows.

- What television stations do they watch?

  - o   You can advertise on major networks or on local cable television.

  - o   You can be on a wide range of interview shows from one on a major network to your local cable television or university station.

- Who are their Internet providers?

  - o   You can advertise on the site.

  - o   You can place a link on the site.

  - o   You can purchase paid sponsor spots.

- What are their hobbies? Hobbies lead people to special events, trade magazines, and specialty shops.

  - o   What events do they attend?

  - o   You can exhibit at the event.

  - o   You can speak at the event.

  - o   You can advertise in their program.

  - o   You can sponsor a snack, meal, or a promotional item, like a tote bag with your name on one side and the event promoter's name on the other side.

- What is their life stage and what events does it include?

Mailing Lists

You can rent a mailing list of people that match your

defining customer characteristic. The cost is from 10 to 25 cents (and up) per name with a minimum of 1000 names. To find mailing list companies, search for mailing lists on the Internet.

Your agreement with the company is that you will use the list once. The list companies seed the list with their own names and catch people who use the list a second time. A second mailing means renting the list again.

Competitors

A competitor is a business that competes with you for your customers. Do not underestimate the number of competitors you might have. You will need to think out-of-the-box in order to identify your competitors. Competitors are commonly divided into two groups.

Competitor Groups

1. Businesses that sell the same or similar products or services.
2. Businesses that compete for the same customer budget item, such as entertainment, vacation, education, etc.

If you are competing for temporary staffing of a local hospital, the most obvious competitor is another temporary staffing service. The less obvious is the nurse who is willing to work part-time or per-diem for the hospital, seasonal staff, an in-house temporary staffing pool, or a travel nurse company.

If you were a legal nurse consultant, the most obvious competitor would be another legal nurse consultant. The less obvious is the paralegal and the physician reviewer.

If you are an education business, any business that competes for the customer's education time and budgeted education dollar is your competitor. The education topics may not be similar and may not even be for the same person in the family.

Conclusion

You are not ready to start your business until you have identified your customers and competitors and learned everything you can about them. Put a plan of action together to reach your customers and to communicate your competitive advantage. Communicating that competitive advantage is discussed in the chapter on relationship marketing.

Chapter 13
Income and Taxes

As a nurse in business, you will need to set the price you will charge your customers and pay your taxes based on that income. Nurses often have a difficult time with this process, probably because we are taught that nursing is not about money and as employees our employers handle our tax payments. This chapter will detail the steps in setting your fees, pricing your products, and how to pay your taxes.

Since small business is so deeply rooted in our culture, fees and prices are also well established in the U.S. They vary slightly from one geographical area to another and from urban settings to rural areas. But, basically a product sells for about the same price across the country. Customers expect to pay the same for a pillow in Arkansas and in Florida. The difference lies in the quality and how rare it is. If you want a pillow filled with flax seeds and molded to your neck, you will pay more than for one filled with polyester.

In order to make a profit, you must determine the cost

of the product (the pillow), the administrative costs to operate the business, the costs to market the pillow, and the costs to distribute it to our customer. After you determine your expenses, add profit as a percentage (20% to 50% is typical), and you have the price. The next step is to take that price and compare it to the competition. Finally, you set the price that you think customers will pay for the product. Setting the price below your competition when it is below your expenses will lead to bankruptcy.

Services

Service fees, such as consulting fees, are more difficult to set and many things come into play when trying to determine how much to charge. It is best to determine what you are going to charge for and stick with those policies when first quoting your fees. Fees are typically negotiable.

Are you going to charge by the hour, the day or half day, or the project? Charging by the project simply means figuring out the number of hours you anticipate for the job and adding them up. Charging by the day or half-day is the same process. It is best to stick with how others charge within your industry. Customers get used to similar fee policies within each industry.

- Does your industry charge for travel in the form of mileage?

- Does your industry charge for travel time?

- Does your industry charge for supplies?

- Does your industry charge by the hour or by the project? What is the usual and customary hourly rate?

Consulting hourly rates for healthcare professionals in the U.S. typically range from $85 to $250 per hour and up.

Consulting daily rates range from $600 to $5000 plus travel and lodging expenses.

You have to meet your expenses and make a profit to stay in business.

- More or less—great debates take place regarding whether to keep your fees and prices low or high. Some opinions say a low price sells more products; others say that a low price indicates poor quality and sells fewer products or services. The final decision must be one that feels good as well as is profitable.

Fee Setting and Price Fixing

Fee setting is trying to determine a fee for your consulting services. It is a prudent action when determining your fees. Price fixing is when prices are set in advance rather than by the free market.

Consumers rely on a free and open competition to receive the best goods and services at the lowest prices. The competition process only works when vendors set prices honestly and independently. Price fixing, rigging of bids, and other forms of collusion are illegal. Perpetrators are subject to federal criminal prosecution by the Antitrust Division of the U.S. Department of Justice under the Sherman Act of 1890.

Most states also have statutes that prohibit fixing the price of a product or service with another individual or business. The general rule is vendors (providers of products and services) may not agree to set a certain price to create a fixed price within a specific market that has an anti-competitive intent or effect. Conformity of fees (set individually) within a certain consulting area is common and is not illegal.

An example of price fixing taken from an archived USA Today article by David Lieberman reveals that in the late 1990s, attorneys general in New York and Florida joined in a lawsuit by 39 other states, saying that consumer compact disc (CD) prices were artificially high between 1995 and 2000 with a practice known as minimum-advertised pricing. The record companies subsidized ads for retailers and in return the stores agreed to sell CDs at or above a certain price. The five largest music companies and three of the USA's largest music retailers agreed Monday to pay $67.4 million and distribute $75.7 million in CDs to public and non-profit groups to settle a lawsuit.

Understanding the difference between fee setting and price fixing can promote free and open competition. I recommend that you determine your fees by the formula presented and discuss the fee setting process with your colleagues.

Fee Setting Formula

I am often asked by nurses, "How much should I charge?"

The objective of this article is to offer a fee formula to answer those questions and at the same time shed some light on the business side of those questions. The services considered in this fee formula are evaluating, analyzing, and rendering a knowledgeable opinion on the delivery of healthcare and the related outcomes to a client.

The fee formula assumes that the typical consultant who:

- spends two-thirds of the income on expenses for the operation of the practice (accounting and legal assistance, office, office equipment and supplies, marketing, professional development, taxes, insurance, etc.);

- retains one-third as personal income;

- spends one-fourth of the time on non-billable hours (administrative tasks).

Fee formula terms:

- **Net hourly income** is the hourly amount of money the nurse wants to retain as personal income. This amount is variable and dependent of the nurse's personal lifestyle and the cost of maintaining that lifestyle.

- **Hourly expense** is the monthly amount spent on business expenses divided by the total number of hours spent in the practice for that month.

- **Tentative hourly fee** is the sum of the income and hourly expense.

- **Non-billable hours** is the time spent on administrative tasks or any time not billed to a client. Examples are bookkeeping, marketing, research, etc.

Formula: Net hourly income + hourly expenses = tentative hourly fee + ¼ of that tentative hourly fee for non-billable hours = hourly fee.

In the first example below, the consultant wants a net hourly income amount of $35 an hour. This is used in the example because it works out to $65,520 a year for a 36-hour week. This is close to the prevailing pre-tax hourly wage of a staff nurse.

Example 1: $35 + $25 = $60 + $15 = $75 Example 2: $75 + $25 = $100 + $25 = $125

If you have already determined a fee for services, do a time study. It can be a simple study. For example, track the amount of time spent on billable and non-billable hours (keep them separate) for a month. This will give you the basis for calculating total hours and the percentage of the total hours you spend on non-billable hours. Add up the total expenses spent for that month. To obtain an hourly amount for expense, divide the monthly expense amount by the total number of hours spent in the practice for that month.

Once calculated and set, do not discount fees. In special circumstances, discounts can be offered on the number of hours spent; but, not on the fee amount. Consider charging more when offering unique services, such as acting as an expert witness. I recommend that consultants investigate using lower cost vendors at least annually. Profit equals gross income minus expenses. When expenses are decreased, profit is automatically increased. Recalculate fees for services at least annually. Increase fees if necessary. Don't lower fees that are in place and working.

In summary, implementing the fee formula is well worth the time and effort. Calculating fees mathematically creates an understanding of the business aspects of fee setting. When a consultant is not able to meet expenses, the practice runs out of money and the business fails. This fee formula ensures that a consultant is able to meet expenses, continue their lifestyle, and operate a successful practice.

The Self-employed Nurse and Federal Income Tax

As a self-employed nurse, your federal income tax on that income needs to be estimated and paid quarterly. Don't wait to report your self-employment income on your annual tax return. If you don't file quarterly, you may be responsible for back taxes and penalties by the end of the year.

As you know, we have a pay-as-you-go tax system in the United States. There are two methods to pay as you go:

1. Withholding method: If you are an employee, your employer withholds income tax from your wages. You file your income tax return annually.

2. Estimated tax method: If you are a self-employed nurse, you estimate your income tax withholding and pay quarterly. This estimated tax payment includes income tax, self-employment tax, and an alternative minimum tax if applicable to you. You also file an annual income tax return.

Good records of the money you make and spend in the business will ensure that you have everything you need to file accurately. The general rule is that you will need to make quarterly estimated tax payments if you expect to owe $1,000 or more when you file your annual return. To figure and pay your estimated tax, use Form 1040-ES (Estimated Tax for Individuals).

Schedule C (Profit and Loss from Business) is the annual federal tax form filed by most self-employed nurses. You can use it whether you do well, make little or no profit, or even lose money. You can file the electronic version of Schedule C (form C-EZ) if your situation is not complex and you have expenses less than $5,000, no net losses, and no employees. Schedule C or C-EZ is filed annually as an attachment to your 1040 individual tax return.

Some self-employed nurses need an employer identification number (EIN). It is a federal tax identification number for your business. Your Social Security number is your federal tax identification number for you as an individual. Generally, if you operate your business as a corporation (Inc.) or partnership (LLC), or if you have employees, you will need an EIN. The fastest way to apply for an EIN is online. You will receive your number immediately.

The website of the Internal Revenue Service (http://www.IRS.gov) has a wealth of information. The IRS also has a business hotline at (800) 829-4933. Their Tax Calendar contains filing dates and tax related information. Search for publication 1518 on the IRS website. Print it out and refer to it frequently.

Your state may also have income tax requirements. Be sure to check with your state on what they require.

After a nurse learns the basics, most find setting fees,

documenting income, and paying taxes easy to accomplish. Bookkeeping software makes the process of financial documentation simple and routine.

Chapter 15
Financing Your Business

Start by looking to yourself. Self-financing is the number one source of financing for a small business venture.

Typical consulting service business startup costs range from $6,000 to $8,000 for a home office and up depending on the complexity of equipment and communication services needed. The table below lists usual and customary startup costs for a service business renting office space and furnishing the office for customer visits, a total of $8550 for a home office.

Average startup expenses	
Furnishing	$3,000
Insurance	$50
Legal costs	$300

Average startup expenses	
Office equipment and electronics	$3,000
Software	$500
Sales literature	$1,000
Stationary, logo, letterhead, promotional material	$400
Unanticipated	$300
Total costs	$8,550

Use the following startup cost worksheets like a checklist. It will help you determine the cost of startup and ongoing costs you will face over the first three months. The Small Business Administration (SBA) has partnered with Palo Alto Software to offer business startup calculators, sample business plans, and other resources on the Internet.

Palo Alto startup business plans
http://www.bplans.com/

Startup Costs One-time Expenses Worksheet

Startup Expense	Dollar Amount	Description

Startup Expense	Dollar Amount	Description
Advertising		Promotion for the business opening including brochures, letterhead, logo, business cards, and media advertising
Business insurances		Costs from agent
Cash		The amount of money needed in the cash register to open
Construction		Cost to build office or plant
First lease payment		Fee to start the lease, often includes the first and last months' lease payments
Fixing up the office and decorating		Decorating and cleaning space, carpet, windows, etc.
Inventory		The products needed to open the business
Office equipment and fixtures		Cost of office equipment, e.g., computers, fax machines, telephones
Office remodeling		Any remodeling done to an existing space, such as a home office

Startup Expense	Dollar Amount	Description
Permits, licenses, and bonds		City, county, state, and federal licenses and permits
Professional fees		Attorney, accountant
Service deposits		Deposits for utility companies
Unanticipated		Include an amount for the unexpected
Total startup costs		Total amount needed before opening

Expenses for First 3 Months Worksheet

Expenses	Amount	Description
Advertising		
Bank service fee		
Dues and subscriptions		
Health insurance		Exclude any startup expense
Inventory		
Lease payments		Exclude startup expense
Loan payments		Principal and interest payments
Merchant card account fees		

Expenses	Amount	Description
Office expenses		
Payroll		
Payroll taxes and other expenses		
Postage and shipping fees		
Professional fees		
Rent		
Repairs and maintenance		
Sales tax		
Supplies		
Telephone		
Unanticipated		
Utilities		
Your salary		
Total expenses for 3 months		
Total startup		Amount from startup worksheet.
Total cash needed to start and operate for three months		

Once you have determined what type of business you

want to start and have a general startup and operating cost projection for the first three months, the next step is figuring where to get the money for the venture. Even if your business qualifies for a loan, each bank or investor wants to know that you have enough faith in your business to put in your own money, or why should they risk theirs?

Grants

Grants are looked at as the ideal business financing. However, they are almost impossible to obtain for startup. The requirements for grants cannot be met by a consulting service or a staffing service. If you have a business that will produce a product that will provide work for residents of a declining town with no employment, you may be able to get a grant.

The Small Business Administration offers some grant programs that are generally designed to expand and enhance organizations that provide small business management, technical, or financial assistance. The grants generally support non-profit organizations, intermediary lending institutions, and state and local governments including schools and universities.

Bank Loans

Bank loans for small business startup are a myth. You could say that banks are prohibited from offering startup business loans by the Federal government. The Federal law requires that state banks protect their depositors' money and not put that money at risk. The failure rate for small businesses in the U.S. is 80% in the first five years—an unacceptable risk for depositors' money. Commercial lending companies have similar policies. Personal collateral can be used to back loans for business startup. The banks want the business owner to use some of their own money for the startup.

Even when backed by personal signature or collateral, a bank often is not interested in loaning less than $25,000. They consider that the documentation and the expense required does not justify a smaller loan. Remember, what you borrow you must pay back.

The Small Business Administration does not provide business loans. They do, however, back a percentage of the loan and make it more appealing to the bank.

Equity Financing

Equity financing can come from various sources, including venture capitalist firms, banks, and private investors, such as your cousin Ernie. With equity financing, you receive money in exchange for part of the ownership of the company. Equity financing means trading part of the ownership in the company for money. The more money you receive, the more control investors take. The question is how much are you willing to give up?

Angels

Angels are people or firms who provide startup funds for small businesses. The term angel (meaning investor) was originally used for investors of Broadway shows and now refers to anyone investing in small business. They are often professional people looking for an investment that will provide income in their retirement years.

Typical angels are corporation executives or professional people who are working with you, such as physicians, accountants, attorneys, or insurance agents. They have an inside view of you and your business and its potential. There is a simple way to find an angel online. The U.S. Small Business Administration's Office of Advocacy developed ACE-Net. Only entrepreneurs who can sell security interest in their companies can enroll. There is an annual fee to enroll and it varies by state. The investors are seeking small, dynamic, growing businesses seeking $250,000 to $5 million in equity financing. Small service businesses and staffing services are of no interest to the equity-financing firm.

Venture Capital

Venture capital was originally a renegade source of financing for startup businesses. It gained momentum during the late 70s and 80s, fueled by the high technical industry. Billons of dollars were invested and many billions more were earned in software, silicon chips, circuit boards and biotechnology. The industry has stabilized and no longer attracts these renegade investors.

The venture capitalists of today are often part of venture capital firms. They expect large returns on large amounts of money, rarely making investments under one million. The average investment is $4 million. Depending on the risk involved, the equity taken ranges from 20% to 80%. The venture capitalist only invests in companies that have the potential of making a large return or doubling their money over three to five years. The high tech industry is still the prevalent industry of interest to venture capitalist firms.

Finding a venture capitalist firm is not easy but some Internet resources are available:

Internet resources for venture capitalist firms
National Venture Capital Association http://www.nvca.org/
United States Small Business Administration http://www.sba.gov/
vFinance.com http://www.vfinance.com/

Debt Financing

Debt financing is a loan that you will repay. The loaning institution or person takes no part of your company. Lenders include banks, commercial lenders, and personal credit cards. A mind-boggling variety of loans are available. Lenders typically structure loans in these common varieties.

- **Line-of-credit loans**
  This is a short-term loan that extends the cash available in your business checking account to the upper limit of the loan contract. The business pays interest on the actual amount received from the time it is received until paid back.

- **Installment loans**
  This is a short-term loan with monthly payments that cover both principal and interest.

- **Balloon loans**
  This is a loan where only the interest is paid back and the balloon is the principal due on the final day of the loan.

- **Interim loans** are used to make periodic loans to building new facilities. A mortgage will pay off the loan.

- **Secured and unsecured loans** require collateral and an unsecured one does not.

- **Letter of credit** is a document that substitutes the bank's credit for the business's credit up to a specific amount over a specific length of time. This is used to pay suppliers and is typically used in international trade.

- **Term loans** have two categories: short and long term loans. Typically, these are written for terms of several years.

- **Second mortgages** are when mortgaged real estate is used to secure the loan.

- **Inventory and equipment loans** are loans for the purchase of and secured by inventory or equipment.

- **Account receivable loans** are secured by outstanding accounts. Often this type of loan is used by temporary staffing services to pay nurses every two weeks while waiting for the hospitals to pay the staffing service. Hospitals often pay every 60 to 120 days and longer if there is no penalty for late payments.

- **Personal loans** include money that is guaranteed by personal signature and/or personal collateral is loaned to your business.   ·

- **Guaranteed loans** are when a third party guarantees the loan, such as, an investor, a family member, or the Small Business Administration.

- **Commercial loans** are the standard loan offered by a bank to small business.

Most Common Financing

Most small businesses are financed by personal funds, such as:

- part of a retirement fund;

- personal savings account;

- equity in a personal dwelling by increasing the mortgage, re-mortgaging, or getting a second mortgage;

- credit card debt interest rates can be low or nonexistent if you are able to juggle the credit cards effectively.

Personal savings is by far the best approach to finance your business. With this there is no money to pay back and no interest to pay. When you borrow money, regardless of how low the interest rate is, it is still money you have to pay. Nurses have an advantage. They can save money by working extra shifts before startup and subsidize monthly income with shift work that does not interfere with normal business hours.

Chapter 16
Business Location

Real estate people are quoted as saying, "location, location, location." The location of your administrative offices is absolutely vital to your success. Regardless of the nature of the business, you must have a crystal-clear picture of what your business needs, what you want, and what you will settle for.

The type of location depends on the type of business you have. A retail store is dependent on the geographical location of its customers. A manufacturer or distributor does not need to be near the customer, but does need to be close to employees. A service business's location that provides local service wants customers nearby, but to a service business that depends on telecommunication and the Internet, the location is not important. Some types of businesses are mixed, and it is difficult to make a choice.

Business incubators and organizations assist with startup and companies in their critical early days. Incubators provide hands-on assistance, space, equipment, and expandability all under one roof for a fee. Usually the time spent in an incubator is limited. Contact the National Business Incubation Association for a list of incubators in your area.

National Business Incubation Association
http://www.nbia.org

Types of Locations

Business Type	Location
Home based	Operating your office and business from a space within your home or on your home property. Some businesses can not be operated legally from home. Space can be augmented with rented hotel space, and rented or sharing office space for customer and vendor meetings. Residential zones and deed-restricted communities usually prohibit home businesses.
Commercial	Office buildings and industrial parks offer space to businesses that do not require customer traffic by foot or automobile.
Home office	An office space in your home or on your home property when services are preformed by phone, over the Internet, or off site.

How to Become a Self-Employed RN and/or Business Owner

Business Type	Location
Industrial	Manufacturing and distribution businesses that need a plant, warehouse facility, or heavy equipment.
Mobile	A business location that is mobile, e.g., car, van, or truck. Most mobile businesses also have home offices.
Retail	Businesses that require a place to sell their products or services. Customer traffic is necessary. Sharing an office space with a business that compliments yours is called co-branding. Make sure to get the space-sharing agreement in writing.

Office Location	Questions to ask yourself
Competitors	Are their competitors in the surrounding area and can you compete with them successfully?
Complementary businesses	Will businesses in the surrounding area attract customers that will also patronize your business?
Cost	Is the lease or rent affordable?
Customer access	Is the office accessible to your potential customers?
Employee access	Is the office accessible to your potential employees?

Office Location	Questions to ask yourself
Expansion	Does the location accommodate growth?
Facility size	Is it right for your business?
Image	Does the area and office match the image you have of your business?
Layout	Does the layout fit your requirements?
Repairs	Does the space need repairs?
Safety	Is the location safe with a low crime rate?
Shipping	Can delivery services reach your location?
Utilities	Does it have existing wiring and plumbing and does it need repair?
Ventilation	Is the ventilation effective for your use?
Zone	Is the zoning appropriate for your type of business?

Home Office

Working at home is a challenge. There are often interruptions by family and friends and personal chores competing for your time. To reduce the risk of losing time and reducing your professional image, a home office should be set up in a separate location in the home and have a separate communication system. Having a child or other family member talking or laughing in the background when you are on a business phone call is not acceptable.

If your office is in your home, there is no need to communicate to your customers where your business is located. Most likely your storefront is not your home, it is your telephone or more likely website.

A home-based office is not the same as a home-based business. The home office is an office separate from the business operation. A home-based business is operated completely from the home. Most zoning laws do not permit home-based businesses in a residential zone. Home offices are usually allowed in residential zoned areas.

Professional Image for Home Offices

Service	Ideas for a Professional Look
Phone service	Have a separate phone line under the business name. Only answer the phone in a business manner giving your business and personal name.
Fax service	Program the facsimile machine to print your company name and number of the fax when sending.
Internet service	Use an electronic signature on your email. An electronic signature is simply your personal name, your position in the company, and contact information, including phone, fax, and email and Internet address. Add one line of soft-sell advertising. Set your email program to print this information at the bottom of each email by default.

Service	Ideas for a Professional Look
Voice mail	Include a commercial sounding message recorded by yourself or another person. Make sure the name of the business is included. Keep it short.
Promotional products	One of the business mistakes of new entrepreneurs is to print their own promotional products, such as letterhead, business cards, and brochures on their inkjet printer.

Unfortunately everyone can spot an amateur.

Get your business cards, letterhead, and envelopes printed commercially. Quality varies greatly. Be sure to look at a sample. Keep it simple, include your logo, company name and contact information. A business card is not typically an advertisement. Keep a consistent look for all pieces. |

Service	Ideas for a Professional Look
Business address	Post office box addresses used to elicit feelings of shady business. If you feel that way, or you want a physical address, look into the mail-receiving service that will provide you with a physical address. They will forward your mail when you are out of town and receive UPS and Federal Express deliveries. The post office will not accept UPS or Federal Express. You can have them addressed and delivered to your home address. Make sure to put all this contact information on your website. Using your home address and adding a suite number is okay. But, sometimes, a homey address is not the image you want to portray for a professional service.

Service	Ideas for a Professional Look
Office space	Keep it separate. Occupy a separate room if possible. The area needs to be exclusively used for business to be used as a home office tax deduction. Also, you need some privacy if you are going to be able to concentrate and get your work done.
	Furnish your office with furniture and equipment that is easy to use and comfortable. Working on the kitchen table will lead to exhaustion and disorganization.
	Most entrepreneurs spend their waking hours in their offices, so the design has an effect on morale.
	Office design is moving away from compartmental spaces and towards large open spaces where a team can work together.

Permits, Licenses, Filings

Permits and licenses are dependent on the business type and the location of the business. Sometimes, they are difficult to obtain. For example, if you are selling liquor, starting a fancy nightclub, or selling pornographic products, permits are sometimes impossible to get. But, if you are starting a consulting service or a staffing service, the process is much easier.

The first requirement to operate a business is that it is registered within the state where it operates. There are exceptions and some businesses are incorporated in states that will save them taxes, such as, Nevada and Delaware. Under ordinary circumstances, you are required to register your sole proprietorship, your partnership, your limited liability company, or your corporation with your state. This registration is usually handled at the Department of Commerce. All states have exceptional websites that can lead you through the process online.

County and cities often require a business license to give you the right to operate in that city or county. When you file your application, the zoning department will make sure you are in the correct zone, that you have enough parking, and meet all the codes in place in the county and city. Home offices do not need a permit. However, many housing developments and maybe all deed-restricted housing developments including private homes, villas, and condominiums do not allow home-based businesses. The restrictions are spelled out in the development's documents.

The health department is interested if you sell food or provide patient care services to home-bound patients. The beverage control board is interested in you if you sell liquor. The fire department is interested in you if your premises are open to the public. The air and water pollution control board is interested in you if you burn materials or discharge anything that pollutes the environment. The city and county zoning boards are interested if you have a sign. Zoning boards set the requirements for outside signs. The state may be interested in you if your occupation requires a license.

You need to be registered or licensed as a nurse only if you are practicing nursing. Some consultants and staffing service owners are not practicing nursing.

The federal government is interested in you if you are a meat processor, radio or TV station, or investment advisory service. Obtaining permits and licenses is time consuming and expensive. Start early in your planning stage of startup.

Entrepreneur Magazine offers an inexpensive state-specific start-up guide for less than $20.00.

http://www.smallbizbooks.com/

Conclusion

The ideal location for your business is dependent on the type of services or product you sell. The needs of a business that offers services over the Internet are much different than a retail business that depends on local traffic. Make sure to check with local governments regarding zoning regulations, licenses, and permits.

Chapter 17
Office Systems and Equipment

Office systems and equipment contribute to the time spent on business procedures. Time is money and a poor system or poorly functioning equipment can contribute to the failure of a business. One of the most important aspects of business is documentation and being able to retrieve those records. Records are needed to comply with laws and to operate your business efficiently.

Business filing systems are different from your personal filing systems or those you may have encountered in the past. Records are filed under what they are rather than who they represent. It is very important to be able to access paper documents easily and efficiently. Filing everything alphabetically by vendor or customer will lead to problems finding records in the future.

The following table is a good start on your business

filing system. It is divided into business categories. The contract section will most likely be the largest because most business is operated under a contract or written agreement.

For example, the telephone agreement is not filed under the name of the telephone company or under telephone. All telephone contracts and agreements are filed under contracts in a folder marked telephone. Place all telephone contracts in the same folder. It is unlikely you will need to divide them further. When you want to look at a telephone contract, simply look under contracts and then telephone. Take out the folder and find the specific one you are looking for.

Older businesses have two separate filing systems, one for current material and the other for an archival system.

Filing System Example

Type of Record	Description
Accounting and bookkeeping	Sales and expense information. Inventory, ledgers, income statements, balance sheets, cash flow statements and other financial statements. The section does NOT include receipts of business expenditures. Because of their bulk, they are kept separately by the year in case of a tax audit.

Type of Record	Description
Bank records	Bank statements, cancelled checks, deposit slips, reconciliation documents, notices from and to the bank, deposit slips and any loan-related notices or documents.
Business forms	Standard forms that you use repeatedly. Most computer accounting programs print and allow you to custom design invoices, statements, purchase orders. Your bank check is a business form. Several standard forms that are designed on your computer can be included on a CD to make it easy to find and print them. This CD makes a good backup if the files are kept on the hard drive of your computer.

Type of Record	Description
Contracts	Include all contracts, e.g., real estate leases, all leases, purchase and sales agreements, joint for-hire agreements, speaker agreements, work-for-hire, author's contributor agreements, association membership agreements, telephone contracts. The file folders in this section will be labeled by the type of contract, not by the business name of either party. Equipment warranties are legal contracts and are filed under the contract section in a folder labeled warranties and maintenance contracts.
Corporate records	Whether your business is a corporation or a sole proprietorship, there are records as part of that legal business structure. Name the folders by the type of record, e.g., fictitious name, articles of incorporation, bylaws, and state filings. Include all records relevant to the legal structure of the business.

Type of Record	Description
Correspondence	Both correspondence and mail you receive are included in this section. Include hardcopies of important email, faxes, and letters sent by mail. Most communication today is by email and hardcopies may be unnecessary for archival purposes. The folders can be labeled by topic or by company. Only keep those that are important or those you will need to refer to at a later date.
Employee records	All information dealing with employees. Don't forget you may be your own employee. Examples are employment applications, handbooks, policies and procedures, performance evaluations, attendance records, termination papers, W2, and any financial settlement papers. Label the folders by employee. Even interviews must be kept.
Intellectual property	Trademark, copyright, patent documentation, and confidentiality or non-disclosure agreements.

Type of Record	Description
Marketing and advertising	Keep examples of brochures, web banners, radio ad text, and other marketing material. Include a copy of your preprinted letterhead, envelopes, and business cards. Keep the electronic files on CD with the hard copies.
Permits and licenses	Permits, registrations, and licenses needed to operate your business. Include city, county, state, and federal. You can label your folders by the governing body but more likely you will want them by the type of permit.
Stocks	Company stock ledger and securities.
Taxes federal and state	Quarterly and annual federal and state tax filings and related material excluding payroll.

Business Office Equipment

Equipment	Ideas
Answering machine	An answering machine may not be necessary if you have a voice mail system on your phone.
Calculator	Calculators are low cost items.

How to Become a Self-Employed RN and/or Business Owner

Equipment	Ideas
Computer	The most recent computer is not always necessary; and if money is tight, reconditioned computers are available. A laptop can be used as a desk computer and be ready to take on the road when necessary. Most experts say you should put your money in large portable drives and memory. The IBM compatible computers are the business standard.
Copier	A fax machine or scanner can double as a copier.
Credit card terminal	Credit card terminals are typically purchased when your merchant card account is set up. E-commerce accounts have virtual terminals that operate from your desktop or laptop computer and allow you to take credit cards on the phone or online.

Equipment	Ideas
Fax machine	PDF files sent by email may soon replace fax machines. An affordable fax machine can be used to send out faxes on the same telephone line as your telephone. For an incoming fax, you can use an electronic fax service. Some services are free for a limited number of fax transmissions. The monthly cost is then dependent on the number of faxes received. The service is almost always less costly than an extra phone line. The faxes come into your computer as an email attachment. You can print them out on your computer printer and receive them wherever you get your e-mail. A stand-alone fax machine means that when it dysfunctions you only need to replace the fax. A combination printer, fax, copier, scanner has to be replaced when one component breaks. If you have a small workspace, the five-in-one machines are a space saver.
Modem and networking system	Internet service has become a necessity in today's business world. Ask your service provider what is needed to connect you to the Internet and to each other within your office.

Equipment	Ideas
Pager	Pagers are no longer needed in this era of cellular phones.
Phone	A phone with a headset allows you to talk on the phone and have your hands free to use the computer. Call waiting allows you to put a person on hold and return to them. Call forwarding allows you to forward your business phone to your cell phone and never be out of touch. A cellular phone allows you to leave the office and still be in contact by phone. The dream of working on a remote island is possible.
Postage scale	The U.S. Postal Service has an online service that allows you to print stamps and postage dependent on weight. An accurate postal scale is inexpensive. UPS has online services where you can print prepaid labels.

Equipment	Ideas
Printer	Inkjet printers are affordable. Look for ink that does not smudge. Printers are often sold at a low price and the company makes the money on the ink. Be sure to look at the ink cost before buying. Laser printers typically cost more than inkjet printers. They use powder ink cartridges that are sealed to the paper with heat. They do not smudge and handle documents quickly. Color laser desktop printers are available and cost effective for the beginning entrepreneur.
Shredder	Documents that include personal or business information should be shredded before disposal. Place the shredder near your desk. Stacking up papers to shred later is not a good policy.
Software	Look for the standards of the industry. Currently, Microsoft® for business office programs and Adobe® for layout and design are used most often.

Chapter 18
Bookkeeping and Accounting

Bookkeeping is the entering of the financial data into the system. It is concerned with entering dates, dollar amounts, and sources of revenue and expenses. Most nurses find this task tedious.

Accounting is the bigger picture. It is the system that tracks and analyzes the financial information to determine the profit or loss of the business. It tracks income, expenses, vendors, customers, and tax liability. Law requires tracking this information.

As a business owner today you have the availability of very affordable, full-featured accounting business software programs. These software programs allow a business owner to track his finances and make reports and to keep track of his customers' and vendors' contact information database, to write letters, statements, and invoices by mail or email, write payroll or use the online services, obtain merchant card accounts, obtain credit cards, and backup online. New features are being added every day.

Setting up the books with good standard business accounting practices and terms makes growing the business easy. I recommend using Intuit's QuickBooks. QuickBooks is rapidly becoming the standard in the U.S.

Don't let a lack of computer skills keep you from computerizing your bookkeeping system. There are many on-line and on-site courses at community colleges and Small Business Development Centers that provide training in specific software programs, including QuickBooks. You have to think long term. If you start a manual ledger system, it is a nightmare to convert and enter a manual system into a computerized one. It costs time and money. Start computerized.

Don't just consider the price of the accounting software package. Consider important issues like the track records of the software and if it is used by your accountant. Before you make your final decision on what accounting software to buy, make sure it is compatible with your office software such as the word processor, database, and spread sheet you use. Microsoft and Intuit are compatible. There are also online accounting systems where you can do your books online via a secure site.

Business Financial Terms

Term	Definition
Accounts payable	A list of people and companies that your company owes money to
Accounts receivable	A list of people and companies that owe money to your business

Term	Definition
Asset	A tangible or intangible object that your company owns, such as equipment or copyright
Bill	A document you receive showing the money your company owes to another
Chart of accounts	A list of accounts used by your bookkeeping system, often numbered for easy use. This list is as important as any filing system. The account names where income and expenses will be filed are just as if they were in a physical filing cabinet. You will need to file them in the correct category in order to find them and to make reports correct. The standard business accounts are listed in a table later in this chapter.
Customer	A person or company who purchases a product or service from your company
Deposit	Money put into a bank account
Depreciation	An allowance made over time for the reduction in purchase price or value of an asset
Expense	An expenditure of money for a business purpose
Fixed asset	An asset bought for long-term use
Income	Money received for your company's products or services or as a return on a business investment

Term	Definition
Inventory	The products you have in stock to be sold
Invoice	A detailed list of products purchased from your company and sent to the customer, or services rendered with all costs listed
Liability	An obligation or money owed to another
Purchase orders	A purchase order is used to tell a vendor that you want to order goods or services
Refund or credit	Money you give back to a customer
Sales	The income from selling your services or product
Statement	A report from your company listing what the person or company owes you, usually sent monthly
Supplier	A company or person who sells you a product or service, also called a vendor
Vendor	A company or person who sells you a product or service, also called a supplier

Chart of Accounts

Your chart of accounts is the foundation used to build your accounting system. It is simply a list of your assets, liabilities, equity, and income statements. You need an efficient and standard chart that is easily understood by your accountant, bookkeeper, tax preparer, or employees.

You need a physical file folder for each business expense used in the chart, filed by the year. You will use these physical folders to file the paper receipts and documentation that proves your computer records are correct if audited and as a paper backup to your computer records.

This list is the foundation of your whole financial system. Sample standardized lists come with accounting software packages. The account names under which the company's income and expenses will be filed are more important than those in your physical filing cabinet. You will need to file them in the correct category in order to find them and to make reports correct. Leave space in your numbering system for adding accounts. The following table is a standard chart of accounts. Your accountant can customize the accounts to make it fit your company's needs.

Sample Brief Chart of Accounts

Since the advent of the computer, most word categories have been changed to numbered categories. Words can have different meanings to different people and cultures. Numbers are always the same.

In accounting, an account is defined and then assigned a number. The ranges of numbers used in accounting closely follow the list below. Using the same numbers and account names as commonly used in the U.S. makes it easy for financial people to evaluate your reports and understand the finances of your company.

- Assets (1-300) (money and things that belong to your company)
  - Cash (1-50*)

- Petty cash
- Bank account

*The numbers following items (e.g., 1-300) allow you to have more than one section for an item. For example, if you have a petty cash account and two or three bank accounts; you could call the petty cash account 1, and one bank account 2 and another 3, etc.

o Receivables (51-100)
  - Accounts receivable—customers
o Inventory (101-150)
  - Finished products for sale
  - Services for sale
o Prepaid expenses (151-200)
  - Prepaid advertising
  - Prepaid insurance
  - Prepaid rent
o Property and equipment (201-250)
  - Land
  - Building
  - Automotive and trucks
  - Furniture
  - Equipment
  - Machinery
o Miscellaneous assets (251-300)
  - Startup expenses
  - Franchise rights
- Liabilities (things your company owes to other people and companies) (301-450)
  o Notes and accounts payable (301-350)
    - Short term loans
    - Accounts payable
    - Sales tax payable
    - FICA tax withheld
    - State income taxes withheld
  o Expenses owed to others (351-400)

- - - Accrued wages
      - Accrued interest
      - Accrued taxes
  - Long-term obligations (401-500)
    - Mortgage
    - Long-term loans
    - Deferred taxes
- Stockholders Equity (451-500)
  - Owners investment in the business
  - Capital stock issued
  - Owner draws, not taken as salary
- Income (501-999)
  - Sales (501-550)
    - Products or services
    - Returns and allowances
    - Cash discounts to customers
    - Miscellaneous other income
  - Cost of goods sold (551-550)
    - Cost of making the products sold
    - Cost of products purchased for resale
    - Freight, shipping, and postage to send products to customers
  - Business operating expenses (601-700)
    - Wages such as independent contractors or consultants
    - Supplies
    - Equipment rental
    - Equipment repair
    - Truck repair and maintenance
  - Selling expense (701-750)
    - Advertising
    - Automobile expenses or mileage
    - Commissions
    - Travel, lodging, entertainment, and meals related to business

- o Administrative expense (751-800)
  - Salaries for employees and yourself
  - Office supplies
  - Postage, stamps
  - Telephone
  - Associations dues
  - Magazine subscriptions
  - Insurance
  - Professional services, accountant, attorney
  - Bad debt that is not collectable
  - Interest
- o Miscellaneous expense (801-850)
- o Building expense (851-900)
  - Rent
  - Building or office repairs
  - Utilities
- o Depreciation (901-950)
  - Depreciation of buildings
  - Depreciation of furniture and equipment
- Taxes
  - o FICA (Federal Insurance Contributions Act)
  - o FUTA (Federal Unemployment Tax Act)
  - o Real estate or property taxes
  - o Federal income tax
  - o State income tax

Keeping Records

When you set up your books, you need to establish policies for how long to keep records. The Internal Revenue Service requires specific length of times for certain records. It is good business sense to keep them as

they are required by law. The following table outlines
how long to keep certain records as recommended by
the accounting firm Waterhouse Coopers.

Financial Record Archival Times

Type of records	Length of time
Income tax reports, protests, court briefs, appeals	Indefinitely
Annual financial statements	Indefinitely
Monthly financial statements	3 years
Account books such as general ledgers	Indefinitely
Sub-ledgers	3 years
Canceled, payroll, and dividend checks	6 years
Income tax payment checks	Indefinitely
Bank reconciliation, voided checks, stubs, and register tapes	6 years
Sales records such as invoices, monthly statements, remittance advisories, shipping papers, bills of lading, and customer purchase orders	6 years
Purchase records, including purchase orders and payment vouchers	6 years
Travel and entertainment records	6 years
Documents substantiating fixed-assets additions and depreciation policies	Indefinitely
Personnel and payroll records	6 years

Type of records	Length of time
Income tax reports, protests, court briefs, appeals	Indefinitely
Corporate documents, retirement and pension records, labor contracts, licenses, permits, patients, trademarks, and registration applications	Indefinitely

Accountant

To set up an effective accounting system, you should get the help of an accountant. The money you spend on customizing your accounting system to meet your needs will be less than the time you will spend revising the accounts. By using a standard chart of accounts and a standard software program, you can save a lot of the accountant's time and that will mean a savings of money for you. Anyone can claim to be an accountant. CPA stands for Certified Public Accountant. A CPA is a person who is certified by a state examining board and has met the state legal requirements.

Bookkeeper

A bookkeeper is a person who keeps the books and does clerical entries by hand or in the computer. A bookkeeper often has no knowledge of accounting practices.

Home and Small Business Tax Deductions

Lists published as tax deductions are exhaustive and can be intimidating to the nurse entrepreneur. Better than a list is the definition of what is a business deduction. The following information regarding business tax deductions is from the official Internal Revenue Service website.

According to the IRS

For business expenses to be deductible, a business expense must be both ordinary and necessary. An ordinary expense is one that is common and accepted in your trade or business. A necessary expense is one that is helpful and appropriate for your trade or business. The deductions vary according to the business's legal structure, such as sole proprietorship, limited liability company (LLC), or a corporation (Inc.).

If your business manufactures products or purchases them for resale, some of your expenses may be included in figuring cost of goods sold.

You must capitalize, rather than deduct, some costs. These costs are a part of your investment in your business and are called capital expenses.

Generally, you cannot deduct personal, living, or family expenses. However, if you have an expense for something that is used partly for business and partly for personal purposes, divide the total cost between the business and personal parts.

If you use part of your home for business, you may be able to deduct expenses for the business use of your home. These expenses may include mortgage interest, insurance, utilities, repairs, and depreciation.

If you use your car in your business, you can deduct car expenses.

You can generally deduct the pay you give your employees for the services they perform for your business. The pay may be in cash, property, or services. It may include wages, salaries, vacation allowances, bonuses, commissions, and fringe benefits.

Retirement plans are savings plans that offer you tax advantages to set aside money for your own and your employees' retirements.

Rent is any amount you pay for the use of property you do not own. In general, you can deduct rent as an expense only if the rent is for property you use in your trade or business.

Business interest expense is an amount charged for the use of money you borrowed for business activities.

You can deduct various federal, state, local, and foreign taxes directly attributable to your trade or business as business expenses.

Generally, you can deduct the ordinary and necessary cost of insurance as a business expense if it is for your trade, business, or profession.

Generally, you deduct a cost as a current business expense by subtracting it from your income in either the year you incur the cost or the year you pay it. If you capitalize a cost, you may be able to recover it over a period of years through periodic deductions for amortization, depletion, or depreciation. When you capitalize a cost, you add it to the basis of property to which it relates.

Intangible property is property that has value, but cannot be seen or touched. Generally, you can either amortize or depreciate intangible property.

Depreciation is an annual income tax deduction that allows you to recover the cost or other basis of certain property over the time you use the property.

Amortization is a method of recovering (deducting) certain capital costs over a fixed period of time.

Depletion is the using up of natural resources by mining, quarrying, drilling, or felling. The depletion deduction allows an owner or operator to account for the reduction of a product's reserves.

Generally, a business bad debt is one that comes from operating your trade or business. You can deduct business bad debt on your business tax return.

You are allowed a limited deduction for the cost of clean-fuel vehicle property and clean-fuel vehicle refueling property you place in service during the tax year. Also, you are allowed a tax credit of 10% of the cost of any qualified electric vehicle you place in service during the tax year.

To be deductible, expenses incurred for travel, meals, and entertainment must be ordinary and necessary expenses of carrying on your trade or business.

Your general business credit consists of your carryover of business credits from prior years, plus the total of your current year business credits. You subtract these credits directly from your tax.

Advertising expenses, charitable contributions, and education expenses can be deducted as business expense.

The bookkeeping and accounting systems are very important. To run a business successfully, you must become familiar with the bookkeeping system as well as the financial reports. Even if you hire someone to do the work for you, it is critical that you understand the process. Successful nurse entrepreneurs are knowl-edgeable in all aspects of their venture, including the bookkeeping and accounting systems.

Chapter 19
Contracts

A contract is an agreement between two parties (individuals or companies) with terms and conditions. It constitutes a valid legal obligation. Typically, a valid contract requires a meeting of the minds of two competent parties; an exchange of something valued by each party, such as a promise, product, or service; and signatures of both parties. Businesses frequently enter into contracts and the person who signs the contract should have a thorough understanding of the content.

NNBA member and nurse attorney Tonia Dandry Aikin, RN BSN JD, is president and co-founder of Nurse Attorney Resource Group, Inc., adjunct faculty of the Louisiana State University Health Science Center School of Nursing, and past president of The American Association of Nurse Attorneys. Her book *Legal, Ethical, and Political Issues in Nursing* expertly covers nursing and the law, nursing ethics, liability in professional practice, and professional issues helping the nurse enter into a contract. Samples of consulting, independent contracting, and expert witness contracts are included. The book also helps the reader understand and locate standards of care. I highly recommend the book for any nurse starting or operating a business. The book is available at physical and online bookstores.

Contract Elements

All legal contracts contain the same basic elements.

- Identify the parties
    - Name
    - Type of entity
    - Contact information such as address, phone, etc.
- Recitals
    - Background or history of the agreement
    - Purpose for entering into the contract
    - Key assumptions for the contract
- Obligation
    - Who is required to do what?
    - By what date?
    - Whose obligation is it to deliver the product and what will it cost?
- Terms
    - What is the length of term of the contract?
    - How will the term be renewed or extended?

- Costs

  - What is the cost of the product or service?

  - How is the cost determined if not a fixed price?

    - By the hour

    - By a formula

- Payment terms

  - When is the payment due?

  - Will there be deposits, partial payments, balloon payment, or installment payments?

  - Will interest be charged or late payments be charged?

- Representations and warranties (an assurance by the seller that the goods are as represented or will be as promised)

  - What warranties and representations are claimed?

  - Are any representations or warranties not allowed?

  - What is the length of the representations and warranties?

- Liability

  - What liabilities exist?

  - Under what circumstance is one party liable?

- Termination

  - What happens if one person wants to terminate the contract early?

- o What are the consequences of termination?
- o Are there any post-termination obligations?

- Confidentiality
  - o Are there any confidentiality obligations?
  - o Is there any exclusion from confidentiality?

- Default
  - o What are the events that constitute a default?
  - o Is there a length of time to cure the default?
  - o What are the consequences of a default?

- Disputes
  - o How will disputes be handled?
  - o What rules will govern?

- Indemnification (damage, loss, or injury)
  - o Is there indemnification for certain breeches or problems?
  - o What is the procedure to obtain indemnification?
  - o Is there a cap or exclusion from indemnification?

- Miscellaneous but important clauses that can make or break a contract
  - o Governing law
  - o Fees for the attorneys

- o How to modify the agreement

- o What constitutes notice

- o Severability

- o Time of the essence

- o Waiver

- o Headings

- o Necessary acts and further assurances

- o Force majeure, an unexpected or uncontrollable event

- o Jury trial waiver

- o Specific performances

- o Assignment

- Signatures

  - o Name and company position

  - o How many signatures are required

  - o For corporations the typical signature block:

    Company

    Signature

    Name typed or printed and the person and the position held in the company, e.g., president

Independent Contractor's Consulting Contract

Healthcare facilities do not hire independent contracts for staff. The IRS and Medicare regulations prohibit using an independent contractor for nursing staff.

The following text represents the types of clauses found in an annual nurse consultant contract. This is an example of a contract and is intended only as an example of the type of information covered. Sample contracts can be obtained online, from the library, or with legal business software. Starting with a sample contract and adding your unique information can save time for your attorney and that means money saved for you.

Name the parties involved

This agreement is made and entered into this 5th day of January, 2004, between AAA Healthcare Facility whose address is 5600 North Jackson Street, Anywhere, CA, 23009, hereinafter referred to as the Corporation and Jane Doe, RN, of 6470 North Main Street, Anywhere, CA, 20042, hereinafter known as the Nurse Consultant.

Corporation owns and operates Upstate Regional Hospital at the address above and the Corporation desires to have nursing consulting services performed for Corporation's business by Nurse Consultant.

The Nurse Consultant agrees to perform nursing consulting services for the Corporation under the terms and conditions of this contract.

In consideration of the mutual promises contained herein, it is agreed by and between the Corporation and the Nurse Consultant.

An outline of duties and responsibilities

The Nurse Consultant will perform consulting services on behalf of the Corporation with respect to all matters relating to planning of an effective and efficient triage department (include complete description of duties and responsibilities).

Location of work

Nurse Consultant's services will be rendered at 6470 North Main Street, Anywhere, CA, 20042, but that Nurse Consultant will, when requested, come to the Corporation's address of 5600 North Jackson Street, Anywhere, CA, 23009, or other locations as designated by the Corporation to confer with representatives of the Corporation.

Time

In the performance of the consulting services, the Nurse Consultant work will be completely under the Nurse Consultant's control and Corporation will rely that the Nurse Consultant will work the number of hours necessary to fulfill the intent of this contract. It is estimated that the work will take approximately twenty (20) days of work per month. However, there may be some months when the Nurse Consultant may not provide any services or, in the alternative, may work more than twenty (20) days.

A payment schedule

Corporation will pay Consultant Nurse the total sum of one-hundred-and-twenty-five-thousand dollars ($125,000.00) each year payable in equal monthly installments on or before the first (1) day of each month for services rendered in the prior month. In addition, Nurse Consultant will be reimbursed for all traveling and living expenses while away from City of Anywhere, State of California.

Status of consultant

The services performed by the Nurse Consultant under this contract will be as an independent contractor and Nurse Consultant will not be considered an employee of the Corporation for any reason, including payment of taxes and insurance.

Service to others

Because Nurse Consultant will acquire or have access to information that is of confidential and privileged nature, Nurse Consultant shall not perform any services for any other person or firm without Corporation's prior written consent.

The length of time that the contract is in force and termination clause

The parties to this contract agree that this contract is intended to be for five (5) years, but the contract shall be considered as a firm commitment on the part of the parties hereto for a period of one (1) year commencing on the first of January 2004. At any time before the 1st of January of any year, either party hereto can notify the other in writing that the arrangement is not to continue beyond the 1st of February of that year; otherwise, the contract shall run from year to year, up to a maximum period of five (5) years.

Notice

Any notice required to be given hereunder shall be deemed given on the third (3rd) business day following mailing of any such notice, postage paid, registered overnight mail to the address set out herein above.

How any dispute may be resolved

For all disputes arising under or in connection with

this contract, which cannot be resolved through good faith negotiations, the parties shall mediate those disputes with the assistance of a third party neutral. If the parties cannot resolve any such disputes in mediation, they shall submit such disputes to binding arbitration.

Income tax designation

In the event that the Internal Revenue Service should determine that the subcontractor is, according to the IRS guidelines, an employee subject to withholding and social security contributions, the Nurse Consultant shall acknowledge that all payments from the Corporation are gross payments and the Nurse Consultant is responsible for all income taxes and social security payments thereon.

Signatures and dates of each signature

In Witness Whereof, the parties have hereunto set their hands and seal the day and year first above written.

Conclusion

Every company, whether new or established, is involved with many contracts. The person signing those contracts is responsible for knowing the content. A good contract protects the business.

Chapter 20
Insurance

How much insurance and what insurance you purchase depends on your business structure and what risk you are willing to take.

Errors and omissions coverage is common for consultants who have a home office with no employees and no clients coming to their office. Property and casualty can be added to most homeowner and rental policies for a home business.

Talk with several insurance agents and brokers that represent small businesses before making a choice. Some agents can group you with other small business owners for a group rate.

Nurse Service Organization (NSO) offers a rider with their professional liability (malpractice) insurance for nurse consultants, educators, and nurses who do not practice clinical nursing.

Type of Insurance	Description
Workers' compensation	If you have employees, workers' compensation is required in most states. There are exceptions to the law.
Malpractice	If you or your employees work with patients, malpractice insurance is recommended to protect against malpractice claims.
General liability	To insure your company against exposure to accidents and injuries that could happen on your premises, generally 2 to 3 million dollars worth of general liability insurance is standard.
Errors and omissions	Protects you in case you are sued for damages resulting from a mistake in your work
Directors and officers liability	Protects your board of directors from personal financial liability for the companies acts
Auto insurance	If your company provides company cars or motor vehicles, you will need auto insurance for them.
Property and casualty	For losses causes by fire, hail, or wind
Umbrella coverage	For liability judgments in excess of your basic coverage
Life	Required by banks before they will loan the company money

Type of Insurance	Description
Disability	For continued income in case of disability from serious accident or illness

Conclusion

You don't need any insurance except what is required by law if you have the funds to pay for a loss or a judgment against you. I recommend having insurance to reimburse you for a potential loss.

Chapter 21
Legal Structure

Businesses are a separate entity under the law and have a legal identity separate from those of its members or owners. The type of legal structure registered with the state determines the legal rights of the business. The common types are sole proprietorship, partnership, corporation, and limited liability company.

The type of legal structure is important and has a critical impact on how you pay your state and federal taxes. Setting up the legal structure is not the first choice to make or the first step to take when starting a business. Once you get your business defined, a certified public accountant or business structure attorney can help you make the right choice quickly.

You need to consider two things when deciding on a business structure: taxes and liability. Each aspect is different with each business entity. Persons and corporations are equal entities under the law.

Most entrepreneurs have difficulty determining the correct legal structure for their company. The problem usually is that the company product or service and business goals are not well defined.

It is wise to make the correct choice in the first place. It is not like working up the ladder. Some aspects of the company can be changed, but often the company needs to close and reopen when the legal structure is changed and new accounts have to be initiated. Even a change in name can mean redoing legal papers.

Sole Proprietorship

A sole proprietorship usually involves one person who owns and operates the company. The tax status is self-employment and the aspects are appealing because the income and expenses from the business are filed on a form 1040 tallying your income and subtracting your expenses and that bottom-line amount is added or subtracted from your personal tax return.

It is especially attractive for businesses that suffer losses and the person has some other income source. The losses are subtracted from the other income source. The person is not protected from the liability of the company. The company and the person are the same legal entity. If there is a judgment against your company from a law suit or a financial obligation your company cannot meet, you are personally responsible.

Partnership

If your business is to be owned by more than one person, it can be a general partnership or a limited partnership.

In a general partnership, each partner manages the

company and assumes responsibility for the partner-ship's debts and other obligations. A general partner-ship is like a marriage and has a high failure rate.

In a limited partnership, the general partner owns and operates the business and assumes liability for the partnership. The limited partners serve as inves-tors only and have no control over the company. They usually are not liable for more than their investment. A limited partnership is complex to design and write.

Corporation

A corporation is the type of legal structure recom-mended by the National Nurses in Business Associa-tion for most nurses. A certified public accountant or tax attorney should make the final decision based on your personal and financial goals. The corporation is an independent legal entity, separate from its owners; and, as such, it must adhere to some strict regulations and tax requirements. The owner is not liable for the debt or judgments incurred by the corporation. A cor-poration's debt is not considered that of its owners. You are not putting your personal assets at risk. Be-ware of banks and suppliers who offer a corporation credit and require the owner to sign a personal guar-antee. The owner is responsible for that debt.

Unless legally closed, corporations continue forever, even if the owners die, sell their shares, or become disabled.

The owner of a corporation must take his earnings out as salary. Payroll requires completing quarterly filings and paying payroll taxes.

All corporations start out as C corporations and later a subchapter S can be filed with the Internal Revenue service. The S is a method of filing your federal taxes. The S allows the income from the corporation to flow through to your personal income. If you lose money, the loss can be deducted from your personal income. The S corporation is attractive because income is passed through to the owner's personal tax return. S corporations who don't have inventory can use the cash method of accounting that is much simpler than the accrual method. A C corporation must use the accrual method.

Business deductions are more attractive in a C corporation but may be offset by the costs of filings and payroll costs.

Limited Liability Company

A limited liability company, referred to as an LLC, is a hybrid entity bringing together the features of the corporation and the partnership. Each partner is called a member. It was created in 1977, to afford a business owner the liability protection of a corporation and still have his earnings and losses pass through to the owners' personal tax returns. Like partnerships, LLCs do not have perpetual life and some states require the LLC be dissolved after 30 or 40 years. Usually, the company dissolves when a member dies or becomes disabled.

Business Taxes

The legal form of business you operate determines what taxes you pay and how you must pay them. There are four general kinds of business taxes.

1. Income tax
2. Self-employment tax

3. Employment taxes

4. Excise taxes

All businesses except partnerships must file an annual income tax return. Partnerships file an information return. The federal income tax is a pay-as-you-go tax. You must pay the tax as you earn or receive income during the year.

An employee typically has state and federal income tax withheld from his or her wages. If you do not pay your tax through withholding, or do not pay enough tax that way, you might have to pay estimated taxes during the year.

If you are...	You may be liable for...
Sole proprietor	Estimated tax Self-employment tax Income tax Employment taxes Excise taxes
Partnership	Annual return of income Employment taxes Excise taxes
Corporation or S corporation	Income tax Estimated tax Employment taxes Excise taxes

Employer Identification Number (EIN)

EINs are used to identify the tax accounts of employers, certain sole proprietors, corporations, partnerships, estates, trusts, and other entities. You can get an EIN by telephone, mail, or fax from the IRS.

Conclusion

Not until you can present a clear picture of the company to your adviser, can he or she give you the correct advice regarding legal structure. Your personal tax situation also plays a vital role in making the decision. Where you live makes a critical difference. State taxes are different in each state. One legal structure does not fit all.

Chapter 22
Business Plan

A common myth is that a business plan is the first step to starting a business and that is incorrect. A business plan is not a plan for starting the business. A business plan is a formal document that is presented to banks (or other lenders) to obtain money.

A business plan does, however, help entrepreneurs understand the components and operational parts of a business. Before you can write a business plan, you must understand business terms, set your fees, name your business, determine your funding needs, etc. The formal business plan is not a necessary document unless you are applying for funding.

Below is an abstract from a study released by Babson College. They analyzed 116 businesses started by alumni who graduated between 1985 and 2003.

ABSTRACT

This study examined whether writing a business plan before launching a new venture affects the subsequent performance of the venture. The data set comprised new ventures started by Babson College alums who graduated between 1985 and 2003. The analysis revealed that there was no difference between the performance of new businesses launched with or without written business plans. The findings suggest that unless a would-be entrepreneur needs to raise substantial startup capital from institutional investors or business angels, there is no compelling reason to write a detailed business plan before opening a new business.

Small business in the U.S. is the cornerstone of our economy and as old as the first settlers on our shores. Those first small businesses had business plans of some sort. The format for business plans has evolved over time to define the most important aspects of a business, its goals, and strategies for meeting those goals in the future. Business planning essentials are deep-rooted in our culture, laws, and tax structure.

It is a daunting task to write a formal business plan. One must first learn the format of the formal business plan and then learn the terms used in the plan. Unless you were a business major or have a masters degree in business, the task is almost impossible.

You don't need a formal business plan, but it does help to put your ideas in writing. It gives you a logical, organized way to look at the important aspects of the business, and to learn the business language.

The essential elements of a formal business plan include business description, marketing strategies, competitive analysis, design and development plan, operations and management plan, and financial factors.

Let's take a look at the elements of a formal business plan. You can write your plan based on this structure to make sure you have covered all the elements of your business.

Formal Business Plan

Executive Summary

The summary includes the highlights of your business plan. What you are selling; who you are selling it to; when you are selling it; where you are selling it; and how much you are charging for it; and how you plan to manage the business.

Company Description

What is the legal structure? Is your business a sole proprietorship, a partnership, a limited liability company, a corporation, C or subchapter S filed? Include the history of the business if any and your startup plan.

Product or Service

What are you selling? Describe what you are selling. Keep the focus on customer benefits.

Strategy and Implementation

Who is going to do what, when, and how much money are you going to set aside to do it? Make a budget and a timeline to keep on track.

Management Team

What is the organization structure of your management team? Who are the key members of your company? You may be the one and only member of the team.

Financial Analysis

Project the written budget for three months for the consultant and for three years for a temporary help service or other corporate venture that is not self-employment. If you are a new startup, the figures are estimates or reasonable guesses. Increase your income by about 5% per year to start.

Conclusion

Putting your plan in writing is important. Your plan is a living document. Whether you are writing it for the first time or updating it for the twentieth time, it means proving to yourself and to others that you understand your business and you know what it takes to make it grow and prosper. However, writing a formal business plan is not a necessary document unless you are obtaining funding for startup or growth.

Part III: How to Keep Your Business Successful

Chapter 23
Marketing

The word marketing has a very large definition. In general, it is the activities that identify your customer or client and leads them to purchase your product or service.

Marketing is a challenge for most entrepreneurs. It is an even more difficult challenge for nurses. We have been taught (brainwashed) as nurses to think that it's not about money; it's about caring. When marketing your products and services, it is about money.

A typical goal of marketing is to sell low value products to the masses. That is not our goal as nurse entrepreneurs. Our goal is to have our clients do our marketing for us while purchasing our products and services along the way. The activities involved in attaining that goal are different than selling low value products to the masses.

There are many marketing approaches. The one that best achieves our goal is relationship marketing. This approach places the emphasis on the whole relationship between the customer or client and the supplier of the products or services, namely you and your company. The same principles apply to face-to-face and on-line activities.

If you offer consulting services, statistically you make one sale out of twenty prospective client contacts. That means that to obtain two contracts, you would have to meet forty potential clients. You must be willing to go to the meetings, make the calls, spend the time on the Internet, and/or go to lunch to meet those potential clients.

Even after you obtain that first sale you must be willing and able to move that client through the development process towards your goal. It costs five times as much money and time to attract a new client than to retain and resell an old client. It just makes sense to resell your clients.

Relationship marketing is a simple process. It is affordable and easy to implement. Technology has not changed the basic concept. In fact, technology has added another dimension, the virtual world. You can implement the customer development process both face-to-face and online.

Relationship Marketing Activities

Relationship marketing is based on the activities of a five-stage client development process.

1. Stage one is the getting acquainted stage. During this stage, your goal is to learn as much about your prospect as you can.
2. Stage two is communicating your competitive advantage. This is when the client compares you with others.

3. Stage three is converting prospects to clients or customers with that first sale.

4. Stage four is reinforcement and creating clients for life. This stage is when you add value to your customers purchase and reinforce your relationship.

5. Stage five is advocacy when your clients do your marketing for you. It is the final and never ending stage of the customer development process.

Stage One: Getting Acquainted

The getting acquainted stage is when you and your client introduce yourselves to each other. At this stage, you are gathering information about your client. Your goal is to learn as much as you can about your prospective client. If you fail to capture the prospect's email, phone number, or physical address, you may never have another opportunity to sell your services to that person again. The following tips can be helpful. The same principles apply to face-to-face and on-line contacts.

During stage one, you want answers to:

- Who they are (contact information)
- What they do (business products and services)
- When they do it (full time, part time)
- Where (location of their business)
- Why (their mission)
- How (method of business)
- How much (fees, pricing)

An important face-to-face tool in this stage is an elevator speech with a firm handshake. You need to practice your elevator speech and then practice some more.

At my Self-Employment 101 workshops and LNC Boot Camps, we test handshakes. Most need improvement.

The following is an example of an elevator speech. "Hello, my name is Pat Bemis. I am a nurse with (name of company if appropriate). I work with hospital emergency departments. I offer emergency nursing certification review classes. I have a 100% pass rate. What do you do?"

Use words and phrases from your professional association. Don't try to reinvent the wheel. It's already been invented. Make it easy for you and understandable for your clients and associates.

Another tool is the business card and is probably the most valuable tool in your marketing toolbox. It should mirror your client and include your contact information and photo. If there is no gloss on the back of your card, you can write a note on it for them. If there is no gloss on the back of their card, you can write a note on the back of it. They will know you are interested in them because you're taking notes. You can also enter information into your mobile device.

Enter all the information you have collected into relationship database software. Examples of these databases are ACT, Goldmine, and Daylite.

Relationship management software is needed before you start your business. However, it's better late than never. A relationship database makes it easy for you to have meaningful conversations with customers by providing you with an organized view. You'll always be prepared with recent emails, meeting notes, task reminders, and social media profiles, because all of these details live in one place.

Your contact list in Excel® or address book software is not a relationship management system. There is only one method to efficiently manage your business relationship and that is with a relationship management system, either online or on your local device.

Stage Two: Communicating Your Competitive Advantage

Stage two is the stage when you communicate your competitive advantage. It is when the client compares you with others. The goal of stage two is to show how you can satisfy your prospective client's needs better than your competitors. You will need to research your competitor's qualifications before you can develop verbal or printed content to outdo them. The same principles apply to both face-to-face and on-line contact. The following is a list of tips.

- Present a professional image that mirrors your client.

- Offer case studies.

- Present business successes.

- Provide your background, such as where you are from.

- Offer your education background.

- Present examples of products (one page) if applicable.

- Present short stories of mutual interest.

- Present testimonials from past clients (short stories).

Stage Three: Converting Prospects to Clients

Stage three is about converting prospects to clients or

making the sale. This transaction will set the stage for future sales. The following tips will help you accomplish stage three. The same principles apply to both face-to-face and on-line contacts.

- Use your contract as an effective marketing tool. Contracts don't need to go back and forth with changes. Time and money is lost during the negotiation.

- Develop a checklist of your services and the appropriate legalese. Categorize the list by type of service so your client can check off what services he wants. List the hourly rate and retainer. Nothing is left to guess. Often the client will notice some service that will benefit him and check off more services than you and he originally discussed.

- Carry your contract with you and if you have the opportunity, leave it with your prospective client.

- The same principles apply when making the sale online. Make it easy. Have published pricing and/or contract online. It can be individualized later.

- Published pricing means that your prices are the same for everyone. You can lose customers by quoting different prices for different clients. You can discount and offer specials; but your published pricing remains the same for all your clients.

Stage Four: Reinforcement

Stage four is the reinforcement stage when you add

value to your customer's purchase. It gives you the opportunity to position yourself apart from your competition and paves the way for future purchases.

The following tips will help you accomplish stage four. Your goal is to build strong emotional bonds. Stage four goals can be accomplished face-to-face or online.

- Collect birthdays. Drop off small gifts. Birthdays, hobbies, and interests are usually on Facebook and other social media sites. You can add the information to your database.

- Discover their needs from their perspective, not what you think they need.

- Provide incentives.

- Maintain enthusiasm and keep in touch with regular emails and if possible, attend the same meetings.

- Keep in touch in person, by email, and on the Internet with sites such as Facebook, LinkedIn, and Twitter.

- Write a blog and be consistent with your posts. Make sure they are of interest to your subscribers.

Stage Five: Advocacy

Advocacy is stage five and the final stage of the customer development process. It's when your client becomes your promoter and provides you the best advertising you can wish for: word-of-mouth recommendations and referrals. The goal of this stage is to build a trusting relationship. The following tips can be accomplished face-to-face and online. They will help you accomplish your goal for stage five.

- Give referrals for your new client to your existing clients.

- Provide recommendations.

- Say thank you.

- Send clients links to on-line information of mutual interest that you have found.

- Send clients personal links to pages that contain articles of interest on your website that are not linked to your public navigation.

- Offer to promote their website on your website.

Conclusion

Relationship marketing moves clients through the client development process and builds a trusting relationship. At the completion of this process, your client becomes your advocate and gives you the word-of-mouth recommendations and referrals. Not all customers will move through this process successfully. However, relationship marketing is the best marketing approach for nurse entrepreneurs.

Chapter 24
Promoting Your Company

Promotion is the act of furthering the growth or development of your business through advertising and publicity to identify potential customers. Given the fact that advertising is expensive and unpredictable and that publicity is free and predictable, the choice to use publicity is easy to make.

Simply stated, publicity is the act or process of spreading information through the media to attract public notice. The media is a means of mass communication that includes newspapers, magazines, radio, television, and the Internet. Some media are directed toward the general public and other types of media target specific consumer groups.

A press release is an announcement of an event, performance, or other newsworthy item that is issued to the press. Most news originates from press releases sent to the newspaper or magazine by a person, organization, or company featured in the newsworthy event or performance. When a news editor identifies a great story and sends a reporter and photography team to do an interview and take pictures, that story most likely originated from a press release.

Getting Attention

Getting the attention of the media, sending messages, and blogging are easy. So, why don't more people use free publicity to power start their businesses? The truth is that many do. For others, personal values and attitudes prevent them from seeking the attention of the media. Fears that prevent businesses from seeking publicity are listed and dispelled with logical reasoning in the following table.

Fear	Logical Reasoning
People will think I'm begging.	Publicity informs the public that a new service or product is for sale. Publicity is not a direct sell. Consumers want to know what products and services are available to them.
People will think I'm bragging.	Bragging is presenting information in an arrogant or boastful manner. The media will not disseminate that type of information. Informing the public about a company, service, or product is not bragging. Consumers want to know what is available.

Fear	Logical Reasoning
People in my field don't chase the media.	In the past, members of medical, legal, and educational associations were forbidden to advertise by their associations. Advertising in the healthcare industry was unheard of until the late 1970s and even now, it is often criticized. A medical, legal, or educational business can be discrete and maintain self-respect while advertising.
I'll end up looking like a fool.	Advertising a service or a product is never foolish; in fact, it is a wise move.
I'm too honest.	The public and the press want honesty.
My services are confidential.	Confidential material is never disclosed. Your service or product is not confidential, only the work produced.
I'm not the sort of person the media would promote.	All people have at least one unique quality that causes other people to take interest. The public wants to hear from people in business, especially nurses in business.
I can't talk coherently to the media.	All persuasive media personalities started their careers by writing notes before the interview. Experience leads to confidence and coherency without notes.

Fear	Logical Reasoning
It's so ma-nipulative.	Manipulate means to influence or manage shrewdly and not necessarily to tamper with or falsify for personal gain. Manipulation can be a good thing.

What is worthy of a press release, social media message, or a blog post?

Event	Corresponding Headline
The start of a new business	Legal Nurse Company provides a Medical Insiders View to Local Attorneys
A business does something that coincides with a local or national event	Emergency Nurses' Week Celebrated by Nursing Agency
When a change is made in the company	Janice Healthcare Expands to Include South Jersey
When an established division is closed	Houston Office Closed Due to Increase in City Taxes
When new people join the company	TV Host Karon Gibson Joins the Public Relations Department
When established people leave the company	Jack Regis Retires After 45 Years of Nursing
When a new product is introduced	New CD How-to Library for Nurses Introduced

Event	Corresponding Headline
When a new service is introduced	Johnson Home Health Offers Home Ventilator Services to Children
When anything happens of interest to the general public or a specific consumer group	National Nurses in Business Supports the Nurses' Walk on Washington
Any news you think will interest your followers.	Vice President Joe Bidden said, "Forensic nurses are a critical resource for anti-violence efforts."

Where Do I Send the Release?

Send the press release to the type of media that has an interest in the event, organizational change, or new product. Magazines and newspapers target different consumer groups. Press releases can be reworded and sent to different types of media and different consumer groups.

Most community colleges have a Small Business Development Center that is a division of the Small Business Administration on campus. They keep an up-to-date list of the newspapers and trade magazines in their communities for small business owners.

Libraries have directories of newspapers, magazines, radio and TV stations, newsletters, professional trade and cultural organizations, and business and consumer publications. Newspapers are listed by circulation size. Sometimes the smaller newspapers are in need of news. The Associated Press and other news groups ask that press releases be faxed or emailed to their regional offices. Many websites have a form to complete and submit online for press releases.

Directories cost several hundred dollars each and become outdated quickly. Go to the library and make photocopies of the pertinent pages. Directories are also available on the Internet. Some charge a fee to view or download the information.

Who Do I Send the Press Release To?

Address the press release to the editor who handles the type of information you are writing about. Address the release to the editor personally by name and title whenever possible. The newspaper or magazine can provide editors' names and titles over the phone. Send press releases pertaining to health to the health editor; releases pertaining to business to the business editor; and so on. When sending a press release to a newspaper and the editor is unknown, address the press release to the news desk.

Format of a Press Release

Paragraph 1 is the editor's name, newspaper's or magazine's business name and address.

Paragraph 2 is the name of the contact person with a phone number and email address.

Paragraph 3 designates when the media can print the story, such as specifying that it is for immediate release or for release on a certain date. The word BACKGROUNDER means that it can be printed as needed and has no set release date.

Paragraph 4 is the headline. Make it prominent by capitalizing, centering, bolding, and even underlining.

Running two lines is okay for a headline. This is the line that the editor's eyes go to first. The press release has about 30 seconds to get his or her attention before the editor throws it into the trash. Look at the style of the headlines in the newspaper or magazine before writing the release. Each publication has a unique style. Copy that style so the editor will feel comfortable and more apt to use the release. Word the headline to fit the publication's style. Make it businesslike for the business section and homey for the home section.

Paragraph 5 is the dateline. Write the city, state, and date of the story's origin. Make sure the date is current.

Paragraph 6 simply tells your story. Keep the tone objective and do NOT include a direct sales pitch. Proofread, proofread, and then proofread again.

Editors prefer stories that cover who, what, when, where, why, and how or how much. Some editors prefer stories on one page but will accept two pages if the headline catches their attention. Editors will toss a press release with a typo or misspelling.

Each publication has a style of its own. Good press agents study the publication and look at the style of the headlines and stories. They look at the articles and determine if they are short or long, dynamic or unpersuasive, a direct sell or indirect sell? Press agents consider the style of the publication before submitting a press release. The press release is then written in the same style used by the publication. A style that is familiar to an editor is more likely to be chosen and printed.

Press releases should be factual and brief. Double-spacing can be used when the release is short to allow editors to write on the release. Cover letters are not needed and often cover the headline that was meant to catch the editor's eye.

Press releases are typically sent to the editor by email, online at the publisher's website, or by facsimile machine. Sending press releases for a national campaign may take several days. The results are well worth the time.

A press release is a valuable tool to gain customers. It is quick, easy, effective, and costs nothing. Businesspersons can use this powerful tool to power start a business.

Sample of a Press Release

Edward Merriweather
Health Editor
Denver Times
1256 South Denver Trail
Denver, Colorado 34990-1236

Contact: Mary Johnson, RN
Phone (321) 888-4501 -Fax (321) 888-3432
Email Johnson@bedrock.com
www.bedrock.com

FOR IMMEDIATE RELEASE

NOTED NURSE PRESENTS WORKSHOP IN
HOUSTON ON BODY/MIND MEDICINE

Boston, MA, April 3, 2004

How to Become a Self-Employed RN and/or Business Owner

On April 19, 2004, nurse Mary Johnson's book, *Smart Medicine Uses the Body and the Mind,* hits the bookstores. Local experts Mark Epstein, RN, President of Epstein Health Spa, and Kathleen Paterson, RN Vice President of American Nursing Agency teamed up with Johnson to present a dynamite workshop in Houston prior to the release of the book.

Mary Johnson, a resident of Boston, based the book on techniques learned during her practice at Boston General and the Regional Rehabilitation Hospital in New York. Johnson has fifteen-years of experience in holistic nursing. The New York Times refers to Johnson as Ms. Smart Medicine. The Boston Globe calls Johnson "a progressive nurse."

The workshop in Houston offers attendees alternatives to prescription drugs and traditional treatments. Johnson's seminars receive high praise from attendees. Space is limited. Details are available at Johnson's website www.bedrock.com. For a review copy of the book or to schedule an interview with Mary Johnson call 1-888-343-7777 or email Johnson@bedrock.com

Conclusion

To bring a new business into the limelight with publicity, you must make a definite attempt to attract the media. No media is going to break down the doors to get late-breaking news of the new business. Publicity is the best method of promoting a business.

Chapter 25
Writing for Publicity

Most businesspersons know writing and publishing articles in trade magazines will bring attention to the business. However, they often don't think they can write. They wish they could write. They would love to be published. But, they don't believe they can write. Each of us has at least one story within us. Writing in conversation style is the easiest writing style because it is like telling a story.

An effective method to write a how-to or continuing education article for a trade magazine is to tell an interested imaginary person how to do something. You start by typing into a computer the words that you would tell this imaginary person. The words spew onto the monitor screen when you believe passionately in the topic. You'll have the average size magazine article (1,000 words) in no time.

Getting the Article Published

There are two ways to present an article to a magazine editor in the hopes of getting it published.

Option	Advantage / Disadvantage
Write the article and submit it to a magazine.	Submitting a fully written article can waste time. When the article is written first and then rejected, the time and energy taken to write the article are lost. Often editors want the concept of the article but want a different twist or angle, and a total rewrite is necessary.
Write a query to the magazine about a potential article not written yet.	A query is simply sending a question to a magazine and asking if they are interested in the article. If you send a query and the editor wants a different angle on the story, you haven't lost any time.

Trade Magazines

Trade magazines target specialized consumers and accept articles related to that specialty. Other publications that accept articles are business magazines and papers, city newspapers, shopper and community newspapers, association newsletters, subscription newsletters, consumer magazines, and today's hottest item the electronic newsletter: the e-zine. The library has directories listing all of these publications.

Article Query

Editors want three questions answered by an article query.

1. What is this writer going to write about?

2. Is this what our readers want?

3. Can this person write an effective article?

If possible, the query should be addressed to a specific editor by name. The name of the editor can be obtained from the directories at the reference librarian's desk at the library or from a current issue of the magazine. People change jobs and often a query written to the previous editor or not written to a specific person is discarded.

Mailed queries should be written on letterhead because it contains the writer's contact information. Queries that are sent by electronic mail should include signature lines as shown in the following example.

Patricia Ann Bemis, RN, CEN
National Nurses in Business Association
President and CEO
PO Box 561081
Rockledge, FL 32956-1081
Phone 1-877-353-8888, Fax 530-364-7357
Email bemis@nnba.net

Article Query Example

Paragraph 1
Date
July 1, 2006

Paragraph 2
Name and address of the person you want to receive the query. Include title and full address

Joseph Katz, RN, Editor

Nurses in Business Magazine
900 West 60th Avenue
Anaheim, CA 33441

Paragraph 3

Salutation
Dear Mr. Katz

Paragraph 4

Title of the article
The title should address the topic of the article.
"Tips for the Bedside Nurse to Make Your Work Easier"

Paragraph 5

Option 1 - Write the specific focus of the article and explain how you are going to handle it. Naming some recognizable resources helps.

The article focuses on 10 ways to organize the work at the bedside to make it easier, as well as, more efficient and effective. After a first paragraph outlining the current problems the bedside nurse is having today, solutions are presented in the form of tips. Each tip includes a case scenario describing how the tip can be used in the real world of a nurse.

Option 2 - Include the first paragraph of the article. The first paragraph of an article tells what the article is about and how you will handle the topic.

Paragraph 6

Selected biographical information
Include any recent publications and any personal or professional information to show credibility, such as

"Twenty-years experience as a bedside nurse and currently working with ease...." Make it sound like you know a lot about your topic because you most likely do!

Paragraph 7

Contact information
Include the website address. Editors will look at the website.

Patricia Ann Bemis, RN CEN
PO Box 561081 Rockledge, FL 32956-1081
Phone 321-633-4610
Fax 530-364-7357
Mailto:bemis@nnba.net
Website: http://www.nnba.net

More about Writing Queries

Queries written on letterhead should fit on one page. E-mail messages should be kept within what will be seen on the screen. The query is the editor's first impression of the writer. Queries must be error free and written in the writing style of the magazine. Editors will throw away queries with typos and misspelled words. They think, "If this writer can't write a query correctly most likely he or she can't write a complete article."

Mail the query by U.S. Postal Service or send by fax or email. Follow-up inquiries are acceptable two weeks after the original query is sent. A follow-up phone call is okay with most editors. Writers often send the query to several magazines and write for the first one who accepts.

The honorarium for an article by an inexperienced or unknown writer is typically $150 and up. The magazine will probably want a signed agreement that spells out the rights of the magazine and the writer. Writers wanting to keep the copyright must make sure the written agreement doesn't assign the copyright to the magazine. Some magazines will agree to let the writer keep the copyright and some will not. If the magazine takes the copyright, the writer cannot use the article again.

Conclusion

Many writers use articles many different times in different media. When free publicity is the writer's goal, a copyright assignment is acceptable.

Chapter 26
Speaking for Publicity

Most businesspersons know that presenting a talk to a group of potential customers is a good way to bring attention to the business. However, many are unsure of their ability to present a talk to a group of people. An effective method to prepare a verbal presentation is to tell an interested person how to do something and record it. The words tumble out when you have a passion for the topic. You'll complete the average speech of 15 minutes in no time. You can prepare an outline from the recording, and then edit, and practice it until you are ready to present it to a small group. You could use family members or friends for the initial presentations. When you are comfortable with the presentation, offer it to small groups.

Speaking engagements offer free publicity for the speaker. Local clubs, organizations, groups, lodges, and associations, community colleges, state and private universities, institutes, and business schools offer information and education as part of their meetings and seminars. Examples are the Small Business Development Center, Chamber of Commerce, Elks, Rotary, Moose, Garden Club, and the Women's Club among others. Speakers who are experts in their fields present the information for publicity and in the hopes of gaining customers. The reference librarian at the library has a directory of clubs, organizations, and associations in the community. Libraries also use speakers. An announcement of the event in the local media increases the publicity. Smart speakers send a press release to the media about the program or talk. Tip sheets left with the attendees of the event increase the publicity.

Inexperienced speakers talk best about what they know well and a topic that invokes passion in them when discussed. If you write out the speech, you'll have both an article and a talk you can use over and over again with different audiences. Never read the talk. You may use Power Point slides, overhead transparencies, or a prewritten flip chart as cues or signals to carry you through the speech if necessary.

Experienced speakers write their own introduction and give it to the person introducing them to a group to assure that what is said is what they want said. Evaluation or questionnaire forms at the end of the talk help you evaluate the talk and gather information on customer needs. Leave a list of the speaking topics with the organizers and encourage the group to call you again. Make a follow-up call to groups to show your interest.

Conclusion

You should develop a database of speaking engagement opportunities that benefit your specific type of business. Speaking engagements are valuable tools for free publicity to power start a new or established business. Send your proposals out frequently.

Chapter 27
Get Your Message to the Consumer on the Internet

The Internet is a vast network of computers all over the world that store, send, and receive information. The Internet has been around since the nineteen-sixties. It is an uncontrolled and basically uncontrollable, anarchistic, virtual world. No one is boss. There are no police.

When a computer connects to the Internet via a phone, cable line, or by satellite, it's like jumping on a freeway that is buzzing with traffic without a map. Online services like Yahoo and America On Line have built virtual villages that include maps to help people find their way around the Internet. The online services are like friendly little towns with a backdoor to the vast Internet.

Google and other search sites have also tamed the Internet by collecting all the information on the Internet that contains the names you place in its search box for you to see on a web page. The sites containing your search words are presented by relevance with a link to the page. You can then pick and choose the websites you want to visit.

Websites

The World Wide Web (www) consists of billions and billions of individual pages much like word processor pages. Pages that are related to one another are called a website. Each website has a homepage and other connecting pages. The pages of a website are linked together so the user can easily go from one to another.

Domain Names

Registering a domain name is the first step in creating a website. The domain name is an address so computers can find the website. The address is called a URL (Uniform Resource Locator). An example of a web address is http://www.nnba.net. The http:// stands for hypertext transfer protocol. There are other types of protocols. The www stands for World Wide Web and is the most commonly used. The nnba.net is the domain name of the National Nurses in Business Association, Inc. Net is the part of the domain name that represents a network organization. There are never any spaces in an address and dots are placed as dividers. Currently, you can use any extension you can make up. Typical extensions are com for commercial, org for organization, and edu for education. New ones frequently become available, e.g., fam for family, info for information, and biz for business. The National Nurses in Business Association recommends using dot com when possible. It is the most familiar to most people.

Registering a Domain Name

Domain name registration is available on the Internet at many sites. Searching for domain name registrants with any search engine will bring up many options. The domain name registrant's site typically has a search engine to see if a name is available. If the name you want is available, you can register it. This gives you the right to use the name. Prices for registering a domain name range from $10.00 to $30.00 for one year.

Designing a Website

You can design your website yourself or hire a designer and/or developer. You can use web-authoring software to do it yourself. Templates come with web publishing software and templates are also available for sale on the Internet at affordable prices. All you need to do is type your information into the template and publish it to the Web.

Professionals who maintain websites are called webmasters and can be found by searching the Internet under webmasters or web design. They also can be found in local phonebook yellow pages or at www.yellowpages.com on the Internet.

You can easily design a site with a little education. You can find the information you need online or in how-to books. You are the only one who knows the ins and outs of your business. It is worth your time to learn this important skill.

Hosting a Website

After the site is designed, a server is needed to store the website and allow other computers to look at it. A server is a large computer. Many companies provide servers to host websites. The hosting companies typically charge a setup fee and a monthly fee and ask for a one-year contract. The number of bytes needed to store the site typically determines the monthly or yearly price. The size of the website can be determined by looking at the properties of the file folder that contains the website. Most beginning websites are less than 50 megabytes.

Publishing the Website

Next, you publish the website, send it electronically to the server, and the server makes it available to other computers by website address, e.g., http://www.nnba.net. When a computer dials up a URL address, the information goes out to the Internet, to the Internet satellite, and is then directed back to the server hosting the website. The website can be seen around the world.

Social Media

Social media websites are for social and/or business interaction and allow consumer-generated content. The sites are relatively inexpensive or free and allow individuals and/or businesses to publish or access information. Facebook and LinkedIn are popular among nurses.

A social media site like Facebook can send an announcement for an event around the globe, Twitter can coordinate the event, and YouTube can tell the world what happened after the event.

The social media sites are changing constantly. The best way to understand how to set one up and how to use them is by visiting their websites. Their help centers are typically good resources.

Blogs

A blog is a form of website. Typically, an individual and/or business enters content (a short paragraph or two) that focuses on the mutual interest of the writer and the reader. This is usually done on a regular basis from daily to weekly or monthly. The content is called a post.

The business sites are a form of advertising that allows comments from customers. The content can be text, graphics, or video. As of February 2011, the Nielsen Company reported that over 158 million public blogs were in existence. Blogs are another tool for establishing a marketing presence.

Chapter 28
Testimonials from
Prominent People

Obtaining testimonials and endorsements is easy. Just ask! Prominent people are also looking for publicity. Unless the person disapproves of the work or service, most people will agree to give an endorsement for your business, service, or product.

When a business associates with a famous person, an illusion is created that the business is in league with this person and their fame rubs off on the business. Quotes by famous people also give the illusion that the business has an association with the famous person. Smart advertisers use quotes frequently in their advertising message.

Testimonials and endorsements should be from people with recognizable names, recognizable titles, or are connected to well-known companies or organizations.

For example, you might want me to endorse your book on nursing or business issues. My endorsements on other subjects would not be appropriate since I am not known outside these fields.

Testimonials are helpful on all your sales material, including your Internet website. This testimonial is an important part of your publicity and advertising package. It indicates that people value you and your work.

The easiest way to get testimonials is to collect them and not wait for them to come to you. As long as your product or service is good, experts in the field will jump at the chance to endorse it. Do not pay for endorsements. Testimonials are not considered valid if payment is involved.

Write out an endorsement making a particular point and relating the service to the person from whom you are soliciting the endorsement. Say you need an endorsement from their field, noting that they are an expert in the field. Editing is much easier than writing and most people accept the task quicker if you include an example of what you are looking for in the endorsement. Most people will accept the endorsement as is, some will add a word or two, and some will rewrite. Providing an example lets the person know the length and content you are looking for in the testimonial.

Conclusion

Collect unsolicited testimonials as they arise and be on the lookout for new ones in all situations. Testimonials and endorsements add value to your work and are an important part of getting the word out on the value offered by your business.

Part IV: What to do Step-by-Step

Chapter 29
Action Steps to Start Your Venture

ACTION STEPS

The following steps will help you start your business in an organized and efficient manner.

1. Determine the product or service you wish to provide. Look over your past work life and see what you enjoyed. You should enjoy your new work. The self-employment options for nurses that build on their nursing knowledge and experience fall into the following categories:
    *   Nurses who provide patient care, e.g., independent contractor, nursing agency, home health, private duty, holistic, nurse practitioner, aesthetic nurses
    *   Nurses who teach, e.g. education, seminars, speaking, writing, CPR, ACLS, training program management, business-to-business, and person-to-person.

- Nurses who design, manufacture, or sell a product.
- Nurses who review, analyze, and plan patient care; e.g., legal nurse consulting, life care planning, case management, elder care management, care management, forensic nursing

2. If you choose to provide a service requiring additional knowledge; e.g., legal nurse consulting, life care planning, holistic nursing, etc., learn the tenets and methodology for that area of practice BEFORE starting the business.

3. *Warning*—after you take the course teaching you how to provide the service, you have no income, no customers, and no business. Don't start marketing to customers until your record keeping and accounting systems are in place.

4. Determine the company's name, logo, and color theme.

5. Write the business and marketing plan. Put your business on paper BEFORE actually starting the business to save you time and money. The NNBA has a business plan template and the information you need to customize the plan.

6. Investigate, identify, and follow local, state, and federal licensing, zoning, and registration requirements for your specific business. Temporary staffing services must be registered in many states.

7. Register the domain (website) name. Your domain name should be the same name as your company name plus dot com.

8. File for appropriate legal structure, sole proprietorship, LLC, or incorporate within your state. All corporations start out as general (C) corporations. Filing a paper (sub-chapter S) with the IRS allows you to add the company's profit or loss to your personal income. An S corporation is self-employment.

9. Obtain employer identification number (EIN) from the Internal Revenue Service, form SS-4.

10. Open a business checking account with your EIN number.

11. Make an initial deposit to cover startup and operating expenses. A consulting business needs approximately $8,000 for startup. A nursing agency startup costs are approximately $100,000 and money is needed in reserve to cover payroll while waiting for healthcare facilities to pay—typically $100,000 to $150,000 in reserve or funding through a funding company.

12. Set up an accounting system. The national standard is QuickBooks. The professional edition is suggested.

13. Establish how much you are going to charge for your services (bill rates). Consulting fees in the U.S. range from $125.^{00} to $250.^{00} per hour for professional services. Nurses provide professional services.

14. Invest in a business wardrobe.

15. Find professionals to assist you (attorney, accountant) and clerical help if needed.

16. Secure office space. It can be in your home and an executive suite.

17. Set up phone and fax lines. Unlimited long distance is suggested.

18. Purchase and set up office machines and computers in your office space. Make purchases using your business checking account. If you have personal equipment, have the business purchase it from you at a used price. National standard for business software is Microsoft Office. National standard for imaging editing and layout software is Adobe Photoshop, Illustrator, and InDesign. Professional editions are recommended.

19. Set up an office filing system. A business filing system is different from the typical personal file. Full details are provided in this book.

20. Set up high-speed Internet service—a necessity in today's business world.

21. Purchase general liability insurance. A home business rider is available on most homeowner's policies for a home office.

22. Purchase professional liability insurance if you are providing nursing services to patients.

23. Purchase workers' compensation insurance if you have employees and set up payroll or use a payroll company (PEO).

24. Identify a background check service and set up an account if you are working with nurses as independent contractors or employees. Arrange for urine drug screen service.

25. Purchase or design all needed forms and contracts. The NNBA offers an electronic consulting contract and independent contractor's contract on CD-

ROM.

26. Design and order business cards.

27. Design and print brochures and stationery.

28. Set up the website. Your website should be a visualization of you and your company. Templates are quick; but, usually reflect the designers view and not yours.

29. Begin initial marketing and advertising to customers in the appropriate media, e.g., newspapers, job websites, nursing magazines, telephone book classified section, and by direct contact. Word-of-mouth advertising is the most effective and affordable.

30. Seek customers.

31. *Warning*: Nurses often open their businesses and acquire customers before their record keeping and accounting systems are in place. When this happens, hiring employees does not solve the problem. Remember, learn the business knowledge and put the company's record keeping and accounting systems in place BEFORE soliciting customers.

Appendix A

Independent Contractor Employer Relationship

The Internal Revenue Service, not by the employer, independent contractor or their contract, makes the designation of being an independent contractor for tax purposes.

In the past, large corporations designated employees as independent contractors to save on taxes, e.g., social security, Medicare, unemployment, and withholding federal and state income taxes.

The corporations saved a great deal on taxes, time, and documentation. The person who suffered was the employee who no longer received the benefits provided by the state and federal government. To protect the employee from the large corporations, the IRS put into effect rules and regulations to define the independent contractor role.

A decision made between a hospital and a nurse, even a signed contract, does not necessarily make an independent contractor-employer relationship. The Internal Revenue Service determines if the relationship is employee-employer or independent contractor-employer.

The IRS determines the worker's classification and that classification affects the worker's federal income tax, social security, and Medicare taxes, and how to file your tax return.

If you think you are an independent contractor and the IRS defines you as an employee, you will have lost all the benefits due you from the employer as an employee and have no tax benefits from the government. Form SS-8, Determination of Employee Work Status for Purposes of Federal Employment Taxes and Income Tax Withholding, Publication 15-A provide additional information on independent contracting status.

Four main points are considered to determine employee or independent contractor status (1) behavioral control, (2) instruction, (3) financial control, and (4) the relationship of the parties.

National Nurses in Business Association, Inc.

I invite you join our family. Talk with like-minded nurses who are happy to help you and happy to have your help. The NNBA is the #1 association for nurses in business since 1985.

Mission

- Provide up-to-date information on existing and new business opportunities for nurses.
- Create and offer business education for nurses to start and operate a self-employment venture.
- Act as a national voice for nurses in business.
- Maintain a networking arena and encourage collegial support for nurse entrepreneurs.

Pat

Patricia Ann Bemis, RN CEN
President
National Nurses in Business Association, Inc.

Visit http://www.nnba.net for details online. Join online or call 1-877-353-8888

Join the NNBA entrepreneur community for the ride of your life.

Membership Application

Complete this application for membership. Please print legibly. Thanks.

Name	
Street Address	
City, state, and zip code	
Phone	
Fax	
Email	
Company name	
Payment Circle one	VISA MC AMEX Discover Check
Credit card #	
Expiration date	
Security code	
Circle one	I want to join. Charge my card with $99 for one year plus $6 S/H $175 for two years plus $6 S/H
Signature	
Mail to	NNBA PO Box 561081 Rockledge, FL 32956-1081

Index

Made in the USA
Charleston, SC
11 June 2012